Witchcraft

Magick

Spells

For Both Beginner and Experienced Witches

An Intuitive Witch's Guide to Achieving Love, Health, Protection, Success, and Wealth

Tracy Addams

© Copyright 2022 Intuitive Way Publishing - All rights reserved.

The content contained within this book may not be reproduced, duplicated or transmitted without direct written permission from the author or the publisher. Under no circumstances will any blame or legal responsibility be held against the publisher, or author, for any damages, reparation, or monetary loss due to the information contained within this book, either directly or indirectly.

Legal Notice:

This book is copyright protected. It is only for personal use. You cannot amend, distribute, sell, use, quote or paraphrase any part, or the content within this book, without the consent of the author or publisher.

Disclaimer Notice:

Please note the information contained within this document is for educational and entertainment purposes only. All effort has been executed to present accurate, up to date, reliable, complete information. No warranties of any kind are declared or implied. Readers acknowledge that the author is not engaged in the rendering of legal, financial, medical or professional advice. The content within this book has been derived from various sources. Please consult a licensed professional before attempting any techniques outlined in this book.

By reading this document, the reader agrees that under no circumstances is the author responsible for any losses, direct or indirect, that are incurred as a result of the use of the information contained within this document, including, but not limited to, errors, omissions, or inaccuracies.

Editor: Nigel Lavers
Intuitive Way Publishing is a division of Hedhaus Inc
158F Brairwynd Court,
Edmonton, AB, Canada, T5T 0H4
ISBN: 9798803416418
Cover art: Independent Artist
www.intuitive-way.com

Tracy Addams

Table of Contents

About the Author 5

Introduction 8

PART 1 - WITCHCRAFT

Chapter 1

An Initiation Into The World Of Witchcraft 15

Chapter 2

The Foundations of Witchcraft Magick 49

Chapter 3

The Psychology and Philosophy of Witchcraft 63

PART 2 - MAGICK

Chapter 4

Family, Kids, and Familiars 81

Chapter 5

Arcane Wisdom: Divination and the Magick of the Intuition 87

Chapter 7

Mantra, Incantation, Meditation 97

Chapter 8:

Herbalism, Herbs, Elementals, Tonics, Potions, Tinctures, Oils, Aromatherapies 105

Chapter 9

Earth Magick: Crystals, Gems, and Stones 131

PART 3 - SPELLS

Chapter 8

Love and Romance 151

Chapter 9

Good Health and Prosperity 165

Chapter 10

Protection and Grounding 179

Chapter 11

Success and Leadership 195

Chapter 12

Wealth and Abundance 209

Conclusion

Practice Makes Perfect 223

Glossary of Terms 226

Reference 230

About the Author

Originally from St. Petersburg, Florida, Tracy Addams is an independent witch who has honed her craft over 20 years.

Spiritually minded from a young age, Tracy began her study of the occult when she traveled through Michoacan in Mexico at just 19 years old, volunteering on biointensive organic farms using permaculture methods. Near Teotihuacan, Tracy expanded her spirituality and first practiced witchcraft, being initiated into the healing arts of tarot, herbalism, crystals, and ceremonial magick.

When she returned to the United States, it was to work as a translator, where Tracy's study of the occult continued. She joined local Wiccan covens and was inspired by the wealth and breadth of spiritual practice in Los Angeles, through which Tracy developed her own blend of eclectic witchcraft with a heavy emphasis on intuitive casting.

Tracy met her husband of 11 years, a fellow Floridian witch, and together, they are raising two incredible, magickal daughters. Tracy can be reached at tracy.addams@intuitive-way.com

To my daughters, Zoe and Julie.

*Wind and Trees
Earth and Seas
Mother and Child
Passion Run Wild
Rain and Soul
The Spirit Whole
Maiden, Mother, Crone
Reaper of Seeds Sown
Nurture and Care
Given to Share
As Above, So Below
These Gifts She Bestows*

Introduction

Witchcraft is a deeply human practice, as old as our species' history and spiritual in the sense of *the human spirit*, that which is innate within us and that which connects all of us. And while the craft has positively exploded in popularity in recent years, it remains largely misunderstood—not only by the public at large, but also by its newer practitioners.

There's nothing strange or unusual about witchcraft. The power to manifest your reality—to achieve love, health, protection, success, and wealth—it's already inside of you, a part of you, waiting to be manifested and magickally created. Creating the life you desire as a witch is only a matter of tapping into your intuitive power. Magick is a manipulation of energies, not unlike boiling a pot of water on the stove or plugging in an electric car to charge it. Witches simply use magick to channel energy from Godly spirits in higher dimensions instead of setting pipes and switching on wires.

I decided to write this book not because I have any remarkable supernatural skill or divinely heightened consciousness; I'm not here to show off my witchy skills. I wrote this book because modern witches need a concise, intuitive guide to developing their own personal practice—a guide free from exaggerated claims, stifling technical tradition, and the same boring lists of correspondences pasted all over the internet, as if anyone is supposed to memorize all that.

In contrast, this book is a path laid out for us, which heads inwards toward our own intuitive wisdom. Along the path, I found deeply resonating spiritual truths and smart building blocks of knowledge to use for spellcasting. I'm here to hand you the wand to start this journey and impart the confidence you need to practice your own magick. Make no mistake: The spells in this book are full-blown witchcraft, and I'm here to prepare you to cast them, translating ancient language into the context of our modern times.

My witchcraft is eclectic and deeply personal, inspired by traditional Wicca, the folk magick of Mexico, Hermeticism of ancient Greece, and Eastern philosophy. My magick is intuitive and green, as I worship nature, revering the remarkable fractal patterns of the universe—from the microcosm of subatomic particles, vibrating with divine energy, to the macrocosm of stars and galaxies, exerting their astrological forces on our lives. My craft honors the divine feminine as well as the divine masculine, embodying universal love, harmony, and unity; you'll find no hexes in my grimoire.

Above all though, my craft is intuitive, and after 20 years of casting and writing spells, I am convinced that intuition is the key. It is not just the rote memorization of spell correspondences, the careful measuring of precise ingredients, or the stack of well-worn reference books that makes a great witch. Rather, a witch is at the height of her power when she trusts her inner voice to guide her craft. My goal with this book is to enable you to do just that with ease and self-confidence.

To my new witches:

I am so glad you're here! I admire your curiosity and your courage, and it fills my heart with warmth to think of all that lies ahead of you on this beautiful new path you're traveling.

It's been twenty years, but I was once a baby witch myself, and I wrote this book thinking of you every step of the way. Witchcraft magick is an inherently esoteric subject, and so often technical instruction gets in the way of our intimate understanding of a concept or spell. So, I wrote a book that isn't just a reference manual or simple spellbook. I wrote a book that will empower you step-by-step to explore your *own* magick, providing no-nonsense explanations, intuitive exercises, and relatable examples.

Some of the more technical aspects may go over your head upon first read—and that's okay! This is the nature of initiation into magick and why Wiccans study for at least a year and a day before they advance in the hierarchy of their covens. You can't know everything immediately, and you'll learn best through hands-on practice—but the benefit of this book is that you can return to it time and time again as you strengthen your intuition and build your witch's toolkit. When you reach the spells part, you will know how they work and why we do them. Regardless if you are a baby witch or experienced like my Elders, you will be able to put them into practice right away. Also, you can digest what's meaningful to you now and come back again for more when you're ready to dig deeper in your craft. All the while, we're seeing for ourselves how experienced witches practice.

As you flip through these pages, please remember to *trust* in yourself as you take on the practice of the spells this book instructs. Our inner knowledge is the true power of our craft. Any doubt in ourselves will manifest and potentially undermine the spells we are casting, sabotaging any attempts at producing any magick. Don't worry, we will take these next few steps together to embolden ourselves along the way.

To my fellow Mothers and Crones:

My hope is that this book will speak to you, my sisters, as much as it will our dear new witches. If you're anything like me, you have an absolute wealth of spellbooks on your shelf—some truly useful, some you've shared with friends and family, and some to give to the next generation when they are ready. I wrote this book to be a solid addition to your collection and one that you can also recommend to your witchy friends of any skill level.

If you're looking to strengthen your own intuitive spellwork, you'll find golden nuggets of magickal wisdom, self-reflection, and self-compassion in each and every chapter that you can apply to any level of craft. I've simplified complex subjects and introduced new ones so that experienced witches also have some value to gain.

I invite you to feel illuminated by the light within you at this moment– I'd be honored to move ahead with you as someone who walked with me before. Let's find new ways to travel together.

I've divided the book into three parts. In Part I, I'll introduce you to the foundations of **witchcraft**, its history, and the secrets of its practice, including the knowledge and tools you need to become an initiate in the use of spell magick. Think of these first chapters as a sort of priming course: we're going to cover a lot of information concisely. Try not to over-intellectualize it with your head; instead, let your intuition take over using your heart. Trust me and *yourself* on this journey.

In Part II, we'll delve deeper into the **magick** itself, where I'll introduce you to its myriad forms and the many ways you can harness energies to manifest your will on Earth. You'll practice intuitive exercises to guide you in working with magickal ingredients so that, rather than spend your time trying to memorize a list of herbs and crystals, you'll learn to understand the language of correspondences intuitively.

Finally, Part III is not-your-mother's recipe book! Rather than leave you with an old Rolodex of magick spells and rituals you may or may not find use in, I've targeted five categories of popular **spells** for love, health, protection, success, and wealth. This includes example spells that invite you to utilize all you've learned throughout the book. Each example spell is provided in a format that is ready for those who wish to amplify their craft, so every witch, no matter her level of confidence, can cast that perfect spell.

You're ready to hone your craft and harness your innate gifts; I believe in you. Let's dive right in—pointy-hat over heels!

WITCHCRAFT

Witchcraft Magick Spells

Chapter 1

An Initiation Into The World Of Witchcraft

"With every spell, we set a clear intention, either mentally, audibly, or by writing it down, and we exercise our veneration for the deities in equal parts admiration and respect."

Witchcraft is a beautiful and expressive means of celebrating the wonders of a witch's inner nature. It is a connection with herself that grants her this magick that she can then use to help bring about the highest quality of life imaginable. As witches, we are inclined to not only celebrate our connection with our inner nature but to also coexist with nature itself in the healthiest of ways. When we see the inner nature within us reflected in the nature around us we are able to reveal all of the glorious wonders magick has to offer for our own benefit.

In this chapter, we will discuss the history of witchcraft and what it has meant to the different cultures across the planet. We will go through a brief understanding of the main principles of magick, as well as the natural concepts that play a heavy role in witchcraft and spell magick. By the end of this first chapter, you will have a deeper understanding of what witchcraft stands for and the impact it has on the lives of witches everywhere.

Magick is composed of so many amazing elements, including the moon and other celestial bodies, various gems and plants across planet earth, and the energies that move through and between every living entity. Let's begin by taking a closer look at the history of witchcraft and the impact that it had on ancient and emerging civilizations as it took hold amongst various different types of people and cultures.

A Brief History of Witchcraft

Witchcraft has roots in the ancient world just as much as it does in the modern world. Everything that a witch uses and understands has come from centuries, if not millennia, of sacred practice between a witch and her inner nature. Ancient practices have become newly adapted into our modern world as a resurgence of new age and pagan beliefs have taken hold. People everywhere have begun to look back at what their ancestors did and how those people once communicated with nature and the spirits. These sacred practices have helped many in today's world find peace, health, and harmony.

Witchcraft is like a spirituality, not necessarily a religion. Religion can be structured and organized, but spirituality is free-forming and constantly evolving. It moves just as the energies move from one place to another and from one person to another. The things that our ancestors discovered and experienced have led to a deeper understanding of witchcraft in today's world simply because of how they passed on their information and shared what they knew to the next generation. Subsequent witches would then add to the collective knowledge based on experience and continue to pass on sacred practices to intuit the next generations' survival. This is the beauty of a spiritual practice, in that it allows for change and progression, evolving as the world around it evolves.

The Ancient and the Arcane

In the ancient world, science and spirituality went hand in hand. The concepts of philosophy and myth and magick were frequently intertwined in a delicate balance that explained the beauty of life and the finality of death. Ancient civilizations gifted us with an immense amount of knowledge about life and how to best fulfill our place in the world. Let's take a review over the various types of ancient civilizations and the magick philosophies that they brought into the world.

Egyptian

The ancient Egyptians believed in many Gods and Goddesses, those who would be in control of the natural and supernatural. Ancient Egypt, a flourishing civilization that held power from 3,100 BCE to around 300 BCE, is regarded as one of the greatest superpowers the world has ever known. The

Goddess Maat held a significant role in the lives of ancient Egyptians, symbolizing the concepts of justice and balance, with the ostrich feather truth on her head. Maat was something to be maintained, which was done by worship and sacrifice in order to appease other Gods and Goddesses.

For the ancient Egyptians, a well-prepared person would obtain an immortal soul. This is partly why the rituals in preparation of the dead were so vital to the Egyptian lifestyle. Not only were the bodies prepared, but also tombs and special ceremonies became fixtures of death in order to help the person move on to the next life.

The Egyptians had a diverse pantheon of Gods and Goddesses that would represent various aspects of the natural world as well as the spiritual world. For example, Horus was the God of the sky and protection. These Gods and Goddesses were thought to have communicated with the pharaoh, the highest position within Egyptian society.

Greek

In ancient Greece, philosophy and politics developed in rhythm with numerous Gods and Goddesses. Known as a place for higher thinking, ancient Greece was hailed as a prosperous civilization around 800 BCE, giving birth to new thoughts and ways of life, such as democracy. The ancient Greeks were loyal and noble people who believed that you could only become worthy of immortality if you did something incredibly great within your life.

Just like other ancient civilizations, the Greeks were polytheistic, meaning that they believed in multiple Gods and Goddesses. These deities represented every diverse aspect of an ancient Greek's life. The Gods and Goddesses were involved in everything a person from ancient Greece would do, bringing worship and offerings into the home as well as public spaces.

The ancient Greek deities influenced the Roman deities as well as Roman mythology. This is because, as Rome emerged and expanded its territories, it began to acquire not only the land of ancient Greece but also its cultures and customs.

Norse

Norse mythology and the belief system that came with the Gods and Goddesses of that religion are as firm and noble as the culture from which they came. Hailing from northern Europe, Norse mythology embodies the grit and resolve that was necessary to survive in such a climate and during hardships like war.

The Vikings, who emerged in Scandinavia during the late 800s CE, are recognized as following Norse mythology. Held to the truth of their stories involving the birth of the universe and the death of everything, we have Ragnarok. Knowing that everything has a beginning and an end put value on the lives of the Vikings, and it gave them purpose in everything they did.

Norse mythology is considered to be a Pagan religion, meaning that it is not just polytheistic, but it is also nature-based. Paganism is as much about honoring and worshiping the natural elements of the universe, such as the earth and celestial events, as it is about the diverse pantheon associated with Norse mythology.

Celtic

Developed from the influences of ancient Europe, the Celts came to power around 1,200 BCE. These people, whose lasting culture still impacts the regions of Great Britain, Scotland, and Ireland, were once thought of as barbarians. The Celtic people were composed of several diverse tribes, each bringing their own beliefs and cultures to the growing Celtic influx.

Celtic mythology is greatly attributed to the druids, who are thought to have created such brilliant and timeless structures like Stonehenge. None of the superpowers of the ancient world could invade Ireland, and it allowed the Celtic culture to continue to grow and thrive many years later. Even with the introduction of Christianity in 432 CE, many Gaelic and Irish traditions blended with Catholicism and continue to remain in place to this day.

The ancient Celtic people lived lives that were intimately connected with the natural world and the universe. They believed in supernatural forces and revered the sun and the stars along with celestial events such as the summer solstice. Ancient Celts were polytheistic pagans who connected their many deities to the fixtures of earth, as with the red-haired Brigid, the Goddess of spring season and fertility.

The Ancient World was Naturally Connected

In all the many ancient civilizations, we can clearly see how they lived alongside nature and connected with it as often as possible. With growth and power came differences in ideals, and the old religions began to fade. Losing this connection with nature and the cosmos has led mankind to forget their place in the greater scheme of life.

We can learn from these ancient people, remembering how their Gods and Goddesses, as well as the spirits of the supernatural world, affected the way they lived their lives. Every choice and action that these ancient people made was influenced by their spirituality practices and how they viewed their place in the universe.

The paganistic ways of our ancestors gave birth to modern witchcraft, a practice that allows us to connect with the natural world and feel the energies that bind us all together. The emergence of witchcraft was a beautiful and harmonious event in our history, but not everyone saw it this way. As monotheistic religions, ones that worship a single God, came into play, the idea of a Pagan or a witch began to scare some people. This fear arose from lack of understanding and knowledge that witchcraft too is an initiatic path of the individual, but in a new world, such as the new colonies of America, witchcraft was an easy way to explain the irrationally negative things that were happening to the presumed good and stoutly religious people of that time.

Witchcraft in Medieval Times

These ancient practices never truly went away, as the ancestors of these civilizations continued their practices across Europe. It wasn't until the Middle Ages that it was seen as demonic and dangerous, with witchcraft being attributed to the devil. Much of this came from the misunderstanding of mentality, as people with mental illnesses and those who were born with handicaps were seen as being influenced by the devil.

In medieval times, between the 14th and 18th centuries, the idea of devil worship took on a whole new face as the notion of Satanism gained popularity. It was an easy way for people to explain the bad things that were happening in their lives, pointing a finger at something that everyone could agree was evil and needed to be extinguished. Pagans and other people who did not follow organized religion were viewed as companions to the devil, and the religious people of the time began to easily blame these so-called devil worshippers for the unfortunate things that would occur.

It's important to understand that this is yet another possible case of misunderstandings where people did not have the real lived experience to justify what was happening with their limited belief system. Instead of finding an intuitive explanation for the things that were occurring, people found it easier to label things as demonic regarding concepts they couldn't understand.

Naturally, we are now fortunate to be employed in the fundamental education of everyday witches. Witches like you and me can practice our craft safely and with much devotion. As any spiritual pursuit requires its own jurisprudence, I have brought the study of occult faculties to the witchcraft embodiment of this book and secured for you a progression to reference what I learned with complete honesty and integrity. This teaching is secret only in so much as anyone who reads this will experience their own truth in practice.

Modern Practice

In the years since the Middle Ages, witchcraft has not only developed new followers and practitioners, but it has also drawn on the many diverse cultures throughout present day and ancient civilizations. The modern practice of witchcraft comes in many names and styles, but perhaps the most common and well-known form of witchcraft today is that of Wicca.

Gardnerian Wicca

Gerald Gardner is known as the father of Wicca. During his lifetime, Gardner was fascinated by native cultures and their ritual practices. He began to study indigenous magick, which led him to connect with the New Forest Coven upon his return to England in the 1930s. Learning about European occultism, Gardner became initiated into the coven as he expanded his knowledge of witchcraft and began to believe that the New Forest Coven was practicing pre-Christian traditions.

Gardner took what he had learned during his travels, as well as the practices of the New Forest Coven, and developed his own form of revivalism witchcraft known as Gardnerian Wicca. Gardner sparked the spread of witchcraft in a positive light. His teachings and books on the subject have helped to share the information he once learned to others who, since his time, have sought their own place in the universe.

Covens, Cauldrons, and a Higher Calling

The new age movement beyond Wicca got its start from the influences of esotericism, which is the belief of having a higher purpose or understanding by means of mystical or secret knowledge. Esotericism allowed people to view their position in their current lives and what they expected of the afterlife in a new way. People and witches began to contemplate concepts such as mortality, immortality, and karma as followers of new age spirituality worked to better themselves.

People following the new age movement also drew from witchcraft magick that became popular in the 20th century, such as that of Gardner, as well as the principles held by Freemasons and Rosicrucians. With the founding of the Theosophical Society by Helena Petrovna Blavatsky, concepts embraced by Buddhism and Brahmanism were also welcomed as a way to help the human race evolve. Blavatsky's beliefs helped to usher in the new age, a term coined by Blavatsky herself (a high priestess witch), as she and her followers took to spiritualism and astrology.

With the influence of eastern spirituality in occult practices at the time, the new age movement continued to spread across western civilization. Concepts such as tarot reading, yoga, astrology, and psychic abilities integrated into the practice. Furthermore, new age spirituality brought along healing on a deeper level that helped people not only minimize or remove their drug addictions with a focus on holistic healing, but also adopt healthier ways of eating and maintaining a physical wellbeing.

In our modern society, there are many diverse religions and spiritualities that people can investigate where they can find their own path in life. This is perhaps the most beneficial thing that has come from the entire new age movement, in that people are asking more questions about their place in the universe. People everywhere are wanting to do good and help others, and witchcraft has been at the forefront of this for centuries.

Witches are bound by nature's rules to help all the creatures of the earth find balance and prosperity. As a witch, it is your task to embrace the anthropology of us on Mother Earth and offer up your magickal powers to coexist with her and all of the living things that she has created. Practicing witchcraft is not at all about acquiring powers of the mind as some people still believe; it is actually about connecting with the powerful flow of the purest form of energy – our creative energies - and using them to make a beautiful impact in the world.

As witches, we continue to search for the deeper meanings in our lives and in our places here in the universe. We consciously seek new avenues to experience magick in all its forms. From the advent of the age Aquarius, the world as a whole is moving in this direction, regardless of religious choice or lifestyle.

Divinity

There are many diverse pantheons associated with witchcraft and paganism, and depending on the practice you wish to pursue, you may find yourself connecting with specific deities or a broad range of them. Discovering who best to connect with and which spirits you wish to involve in your practice is a highly personal decision. Understanding yourself is your first step in knowing which path to take in this spiritual journey. For now, let's discuss some of the major and most well-known deities and pantheons so that you can familiarize yourself with concepts and beliefs that most witches are familiar with.

The Triple Goddess

As a part of the resurgence of the new age movement in modern times, the Triple Goddess is a vital part of many paganism and witchcraft rituals. The Triple Goddess represents three aspects of feminine energy, the Maiden, the Mother, and the Crone. The Maiden is typically seen as a youthful girl who has yet to have children. The Mother is, of course, a motherly figure actively participating in her children's lives, while the Crone is a grandmother figure who is also seen as a wise and experienced woman.

The Triple Goddess is a somewhat new construction of the three female energies, as neopagan folklorist Robert Graves idealized these three figures as a single Goddess. Aside from Graves, the way that modern witches have embraced the Triple Goddess is often attributed to the feminist movement, in which women find strength in who they are and ask for respect and equal rights over their lives and their bodies. The Triple Goddess is a symbol of feminism because it embodies all three stages of a woman's life, and it also embraces the most beautiful and valued components of these stages.

The Crone, for example, is sought after for her wisdom and advice by many young witches, especially those who are asking the spirits for guidance when they have no one else to turn to. The Mother nurtures and heals her children and provides lessons for other women who are newly experiencing motherhood. And the Maiden is perhaps a symbol of reflection, allowing witches to look back on the innocence and purity of a carefree life they once lived whimsically within. All of these aspects form the Triple Goddess, and she gives strength and value to all that a witch does.

The Great Horned God

As the counterpart to the Triple Goddess, the Horned God is a masculine energy that balances the feminine in the universe. Just as the Triple

Goddess, in her three singular forms, has her roots in ancient civilizations, the Horned God was discovered in the caves of France from the paleolithic times. The images painted in the caves may very well date back over 15,000 years ago, solidifying paganism as one of the oldest forms of spirituality.

The Horned God embodies all aspects of masculinity, such as power and strength. He is known for being connected to material wealth as well as life and fertility. In each major pantheon, we can find a symbol of the Horned God, such as Osiris of Egypt and Cernunnos of the Celts. These different deities exhibit, much in the same way that the Triple Goddess is a combination of feminine aspects, to create the single representation of masculine energy in the Horned God.

The Triple Goddess and the Horned God work together to bring us the wheel of the year. This is the cycle of seasons and never-ending time that continues throughout nature. Modern Neopagans and Wiccans often believe that the Horned God dies in autumn, thus allowing the winter to come as life goes quiet. The Horned God is then revived in the spring in order to imbue the Triple Goddess with flourishing life and abundant warmth.

The Horned God is a strong symbol of the forest in which he protects wild and untamed vegetation. Because he is associated with the stag, he is most commonly shown with his horns or antlers, thus representing virility to the Triple Goddess's fertility. While Baphomet has been depicted in many different ways, one popular way is to show him with the face of a goat with horns. Although this Deity is dark and seen in imagery associated with the Knights Templar, he is also found to be with a human body, symbolizing his dominion over his animal instincts. The Horned God is directly related to Pan, the Greek God of the wild. As with Osiris and Cernunnos, Pan is directly connected with the masculine embodiment of the Horned God.

The World's Gods and Goddesses

It may be enough for you to follow and seek guidance from the Triple Goddess and the Grand Horned God, but some people want to connect directly with specific Gods and Goddesses. You may want to choose a Deity that best suits where you are in your life and the troubles that you are facing and need guidance on. You may also decide, for example, that your style of witchcraft is more plant-based and focused on healing herbs, and that you would like to pray to a Goddess that is known for cultivating these herbs. In this case, finding a specific entity that you can communicate with could be very rewarding in your daily practice.

Because there are thousands of diverse Gods and Goddesses, as well as supernatural entities that you can communicate with in your daily practice, you can find guidance on many different topics as you perform magickal spells. Calling upon the favor of a specific Goddess, for example, may grant you occult faculties important to the work you are performing in your spell. This could make a difference in whether or not the spell is successful, as you are summoning the Deity to channel your creative energy through their Masterful, God-like spirit.

Here, we will go over a few different pantheons and their most well-known Gods and Goddesses, but there truly are thousands of Deities across the planets of our galaxy. There are Deities who reside in Venus and will provide you with healing powers specific to your needs should you know how to call upon them. Witchcraft is lovely in that it allows you to truly find yourself and what it is you connect with, making you feel even more enlightened and fulfilled than ever before.

Egyptian Pantheon

Ancient Egyptian Gods and Goddesses are a part of the overall pantheon in Egyptian culture. Some of these Gods and Goddesses are primordial, which means that they connect with the basic energies that we see in our everyday life, such as air and sky. Beyond the primordial, we see the main Gods and Goddesses that are birthed out of creation, and then their children come next. After these family trees expand, there are countless other Gods and Goddesses, as well as spirits and entities that play into the overall mythology associated with ancient Egypt.

Osiris is best known as the Lord of the Underworld, and he was married to his sister Isis. As the Goddess of the Moon, Isis is a healing Goddess who protects mothers and their children. Osiris is said to have been murdered by his younger brother Set, but his wife brought him back to life. Osiris and Isis had a son named Horus, who became a sky God in the shape of a falcon.

Hathor is the Goddess associated with beauty and love, as well as music. Bastet is a Goddess who took the shape of a cat or lioness. She is a ferocious protector, and she is the daughter of Isis and Ra, the Sun God.

Amun, an air God who is one of the original and primordial Gods in Egyptian culture, later merged with the Sun God to create Amun-Ra.

Anubis was once the God of the Dead, but some traditions have Osiris replacing Anubis after the end of the Old Kingdom.

Thoth is a God associated with mathematics and knowledge. He was often depicted as an Ibis bird in artwork.

Heka is the God of medicine and magick, and he, like Amun, was an ancient and primordial God.

These are only a few of the main Gods and Goddesses associated with ancient Egyptian culture, and as time went on and the kingdoms evolved, some Gods were replaced with others who held essentially the same role. Some Pharaohs favored certain Gods and Goddesses over others, and at one point, during the reign of Akhenaten, tributes to the many Gods were destroyed as focus went to a single and all-powerful God named Aten.

Ancient Greek Pantheon

The ancient Greek pantheon, much like the ancient Egyptian pantheon, is constructed of several different groupings of Gods based on the timeline in which they came from creation. Just like other grand ancient civilizations, the ancient Greek pantheon begins with primordial Gods and then continues through the creation of the parent Gods. With the children of these parent Gods, the pantheon begins to expand vastly, covering all aspects of life through Gods, Demigods, and other supernatural and paranormal entities.

The primordial Gods govern concepts such as time, night and day, the sea, and the sky, to name a few. Gaia is the Greek Goddess of the earth, for example. She is nurturing and protective, giving birth to all that is on the earth. She and the sky God Uranus created the Titans, the Parent Gods of the Gods of Olympus.

Of the Titan Gods, Atlas is known to carry the earth and the heavens on his shoulders, a punishment brought by Zeus after their Great War. Oceanus, another Titan, is said to encompass the earth with his waters. The ancient Greeks believed that the earth was flat, and that it was surrounded in its entirety by Oceanus' waters. Prometheus, who was the God of Foresight, was asked to create mankind out of clay. He is also known for bringing fire to mankind, even after Zeus forbade it, thus granting him the additional name of God of Fire.

Kronos, the God of Time, is another important Titan God, and the Father of Zeus and the Olympians. Kronos is known for overthrowing his father, Uranus, and taking the throne for himself. He was given a prophecy that his own child would do the same to him, which led him to swallow all of the Olympian Gods that he created with Rhea, his older sister.

Zeus is the God of the Sky, controlling the weather as he inflicts law and order. Athena is the Goddess of War, noble and loyal to her cause. Aphrodite is the Goddess of Procreation, holding beauty and love in high regard. Poseidon is the God of the Sea, as well as earthquakes and floods. Artemis is the Goddess of the Wilderness, protecting wildlife animals and the forest in which they live. Apollo is the God of Music, inciting poetry and prophecies to humankind. Hades is the God of the Underworld, ruling over the dead as well as the riches that lie deep within the earth.

Norse Mythology Pantheon

Norse mythology stems from the rigid and gritty nature of life in northern Europe during the Middle Ages. The Vikings, who were the people that followed Norse mythology as a religion, embraced the world for what it was instead of seeking to be redeemed from the troubles therein. Throughout the Norse mythology pantheon, we find Gods and Goddesses, as well as supernatural entities, who are just as real as the people who believed in them. They have flaws and they struggle, and when they rise to victory, their followers find victory as well.

Odin is perhaps the most well-known of the Norse Gods and Goddesses. He is considered the Father of the Gods and Goddesses, and he is wise and just. His sons Thor and Loki are the Gods of thunder and mischief, respectively. Though these two brothers are sometimes at odds, they are both deeply flawed and worthy of redemption. Their mother, the sorcerer Goddess Frigg, is known to be nurturing and protective, much like other female Deities across the globe. Heimdall is a watcher who is both loyal and honorable, and Tyr is the God of Law. These, as well as countless others, make up the Aesir tribe.

The Vanir Gods and Goddess are similar to the primordial Deities in ancient Greek and Egyptian mythology. These include beings who are connected to nature on every possible level. Freya, for example, is the Goddess of Love and War, making her a fierce protector as much as a loving mother. Freya's brother Freyr is the God of Health and Abundance. He is a symbol of fertility and good fortunes for the home and family. Their Father is Njord, a God connected with the sea and the wind. His wife, and Freya and Freyr's mother, is the Goddess Nerthus, a Deity connected to prosperity and peace.

Celtic Pantheon

The Celtic pantheon is full of strong-willed and powerful Gods and Goddesses who ferociously defended their territories in battle. Similar to the Gods and Goddesses of Norse mythology, these Celtic Deities are symbols of strength and endurance, especially in the face of an ever-changing and harsh time in human history.

Morrigan is one of the best-known Goddesses, sometimes referred to as the Great Queen, or the Goddess of War. She presided over many battles, often taking the form of a crow or a raven. Angus, the God of Love, is known to have searched the entirety of Ireland for a maiden of unmatched beauty. After finding his love, and discovering she was fated to be turned into a swan, he transformed himself into a swan to spend eternity with her. The Goddess Danu is said to be an all-powerful Deity and matriarch of the Irish Gods. Dagda, known as the Good God, is strong and just in his actions.

Brigid, directly connected to the arrival of spring and the notions of fertility and creation, is the Goddess of Fire. Cernunnos, whom we have already discussed as an inspiration for the Horned God, is the God of Wealth. Whether it be abundance in the home or by material goods, Cernunnos is at the forefront. Arawn is the God of the Underworld, controlling darkness and presiding over death.

The Influence of Deities on Witchcraft

As we discussed, incorporating certain Deities that you feel connected with can help boost your energies and increase the likelihood of your rituals and spellcasting to succeed. In everything a witch does, there is a good measure of faith involved. This faith is not only necessary for the witch herself, but also of the ingredients and components that she is using during her practice. When a witch can connect directly with a God or Goddess during a spell, then she can trust in her energy more than if she were to perform the spell on her own. Witchcraft is about connecting with everything that nature has to offer as we work to find balance and unity through the practice of casting spells.

The Tree of Life

All throughout history, various cultures have used the tree of life as a map for initiation into higher forms of witchcraft. The tree of knowledge shares with it the same root. When the knowledge of the powers behind witchcraft is respected, the map to higher levels of initiation will be revealed to the witch. Not only does the tree of life support the lifelong pathway of witchcraft, but it protects the witch from straying into evil, dark, black magick. Instead, we proceed as the Gods and Goddesses would.

This Tree is usually referred to as the Kabbalisitc tree of life, and it has three pillars. One pillar, on the right, is for severity, representing masculine energies. The one on the left is for mercy, and represents feminine energies. The balanced pillar is known to be neutral and represents the harmony of masculine and feminine energy. Within these pillars are spheres that illuminate the soul's journey through life. The achievement and passing from one sphere to the next through all ten represents the gaining of virtues on the path of enlightenment. An enlightened witch is an intuitive witch. Just as she has ten fingers, she also has ten echelons of advancement in her lifelong practice. The entire tree is unified from the foundation to the crown, and the pillars work together to build lessons and help a witch grow.

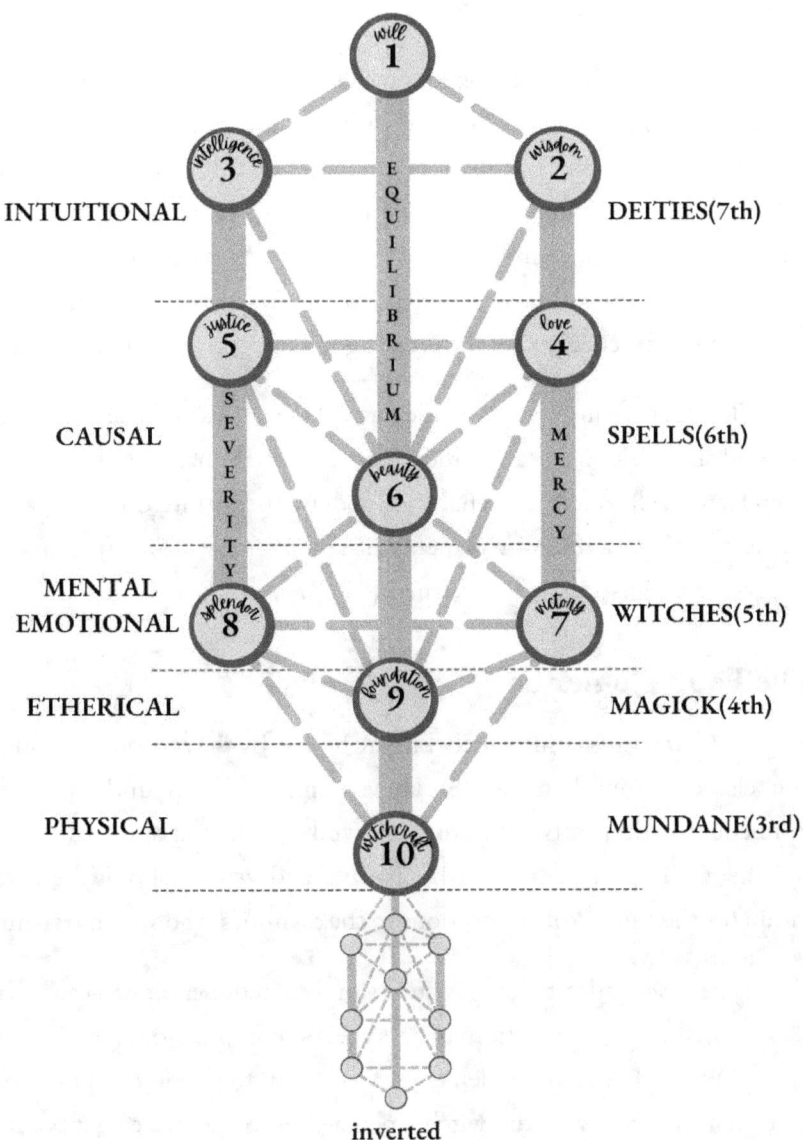

The Magick in Nature

Everywhere we look, there is magick throughout the natural world. As a witch, you may already be in tune with the forces of nature and how they influence everyday life. You may get excited when there are thunderstorms or feel convicted when you choose to eat meat, both of which prove your deep connection with the energies across our planet. Witches not only have the ability to connect with everything in the natural world, but they learn to manipulate these energies for the greater good of everyone and everything.

There are many aspects to the natural world that we use when crafting spells. Plants, celestial events, and non-harmful animal offerings, such as a fallen feather, all combine to enable us to draw energy into our spell work. Of the many things across our planet, perhaps the most powerful category of energy-filled items are the four elements.

The Four Elements

All our spells within witchcraft are bound by the attributes of our great four elements found in nature. These elements, when understood to be represented within ourselves, are both symbolically and spiritually essential ingredients. The elements—earth, air, fire, and water—should be heralded within for their mystical connections to the divinities who worship them.

The basic understanding is quite simple in representation–each element is associated with a direction on a type of compass, or a point on the pentagram, with the fifth element of ether at the topmost point of the pentagram. In this way, the witch's pentagram, or pentacle, symbolizes the union within the universe as a connection between the material and spiritual planes. We say, "as above, so below," so as to recognize that as we progress towards higher planes of consciousness, we unite with the Deities who entrusted us with their powers. The pentagram is sometimes reversed or seen inverted, which represents the triumph of the material *over* the spiritual, as if to say, no deity can be found to help answer the call all the time, and we will have to rely on our own divine intuition. However, let yourself not be fooled by the respect we need to offer the material world as we remember the initiations to higher magick are not realized overnight. Instead, we need to learn to face the inevitable descent into the infra dimensions of nature. We do this with the help of the elements.

There are many fantastic ways to incorporate the elements into your practice. Depending on the spell that you are trying to work, you may lean toward using a specific element as an energy source. For example, Earth is an element associated with abundance and prosperity. If you are performing a spell to help you be more successful in your career, utilizing the element of earth can provide you with additional positive energy that is directly related to the outcome that you were hoping for.

In addition to using the elements for spellcasting, witches adorn their homes and altars with representations of the elements. Certain Deities are associated with specific elements, and if you are calling upon one of those Deities, it is wise to offer them the things that they are directly connected to. This shows that you respect those Deities, and that you are willing to go out of your way to provide them with something they would appreciate.

In addition, our elements have correspondences, which are wonderful ways to link energies together and boost the potential for success when casting spells and conducting rituals. For example, the element of fire is associated with the cardinal direction of the south. If using the element of fire in your spell is necessary, then you could also face the south as you speak your words and make your intentions known. Initiations into the major occult mysteries of witchcraft are often faced through the element of fire.

Let's take a look at some of the other correspondences that go along with these elements. Because the elements are such an important part of witchcraft, understanding them fully will help you craft spells and rituals with ease.

EARTH

Earth is grounding, stable, and protective. like the fruits of the field, this element bears abundant gifts in the material realm, from the precious ores that form the basis of our monetary systems to the sprawling greenery of field, forest, and jungle. It is a feminine, yin energy, but make no mistake; earth is a force to be reckoned with. With the weight of the world on its shoulders, one seismic shift in this element can bring great change to your life.

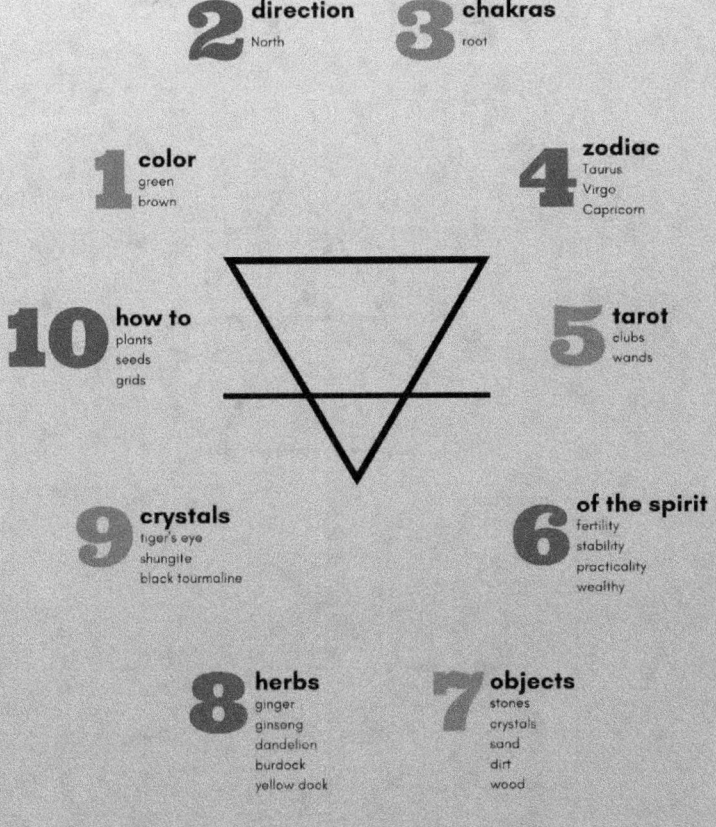

2 direction
North

3 chakras
root

1 color
green
brown

4 zodiac
Taurus
Virgo
Capricorn

10 how to
plants
seeds
grids

5 tarot
clubs
wands

9 crystals
tiger's eye
shungite
black tourmaline

6 of the spirit
fertility
stability
practicality
wealthy

8 herbs
ginger
ginseng
dandelion
burdock
yellow dock

7 objects
stones
crystals
sand
dirt
wood

AIR

The air around us is invisible and intangible but ever-present. While the air can feel still enough that, and we might even notice it—in truth, air is constantly in motion. This motion carries thoughts and ideas swiftly through the universe, so it's no surprise the element of air represents intellect, communication, and change. Air has a masculine energy and can be as forceful as a great tornado or as mentally revitalizing as a gentle breeze.

2 direction
East

chakras
heart

color
yellow
purple

4 zodiac
Gemini
Libra
Aquarius

10 how to
sound
smoke
steam
wind

tarot
pentacles
diamonds

crystals
jade
peridot
moldavite
watermelon tourmaline
green calcite
chrysoprase

6 of the spirit
intellect
communication
swiftness
power

8 herbs
fennel
cilantro
lemongrass
marjoram
peppermint
lavender
rosemary

objects
incense
feather
empty jar
bell
chime

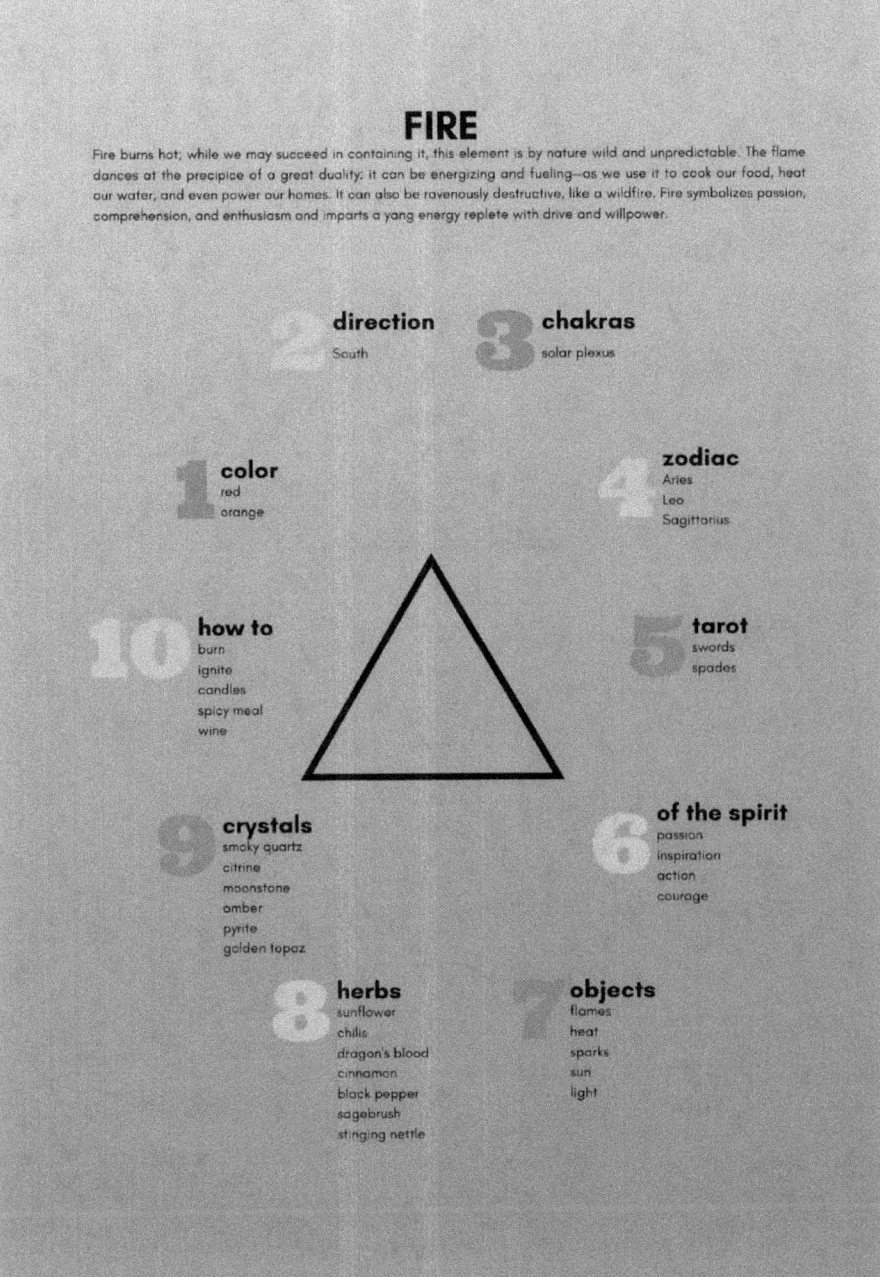

Witchcraft Magick Spells

WATER

The fluid, feminine element of water goes with the flow. At times, water is formatively powerful, like the rushing river carves the canyon of rock—but it can also be gentle, like sea waves rolling over a sandy beach. Human beings are made principally of water, and this element represents our fluid feelings, our intuition, and our creative juices. Water is the cleanser of all the elements and lends itself well to healing and purifying magick.

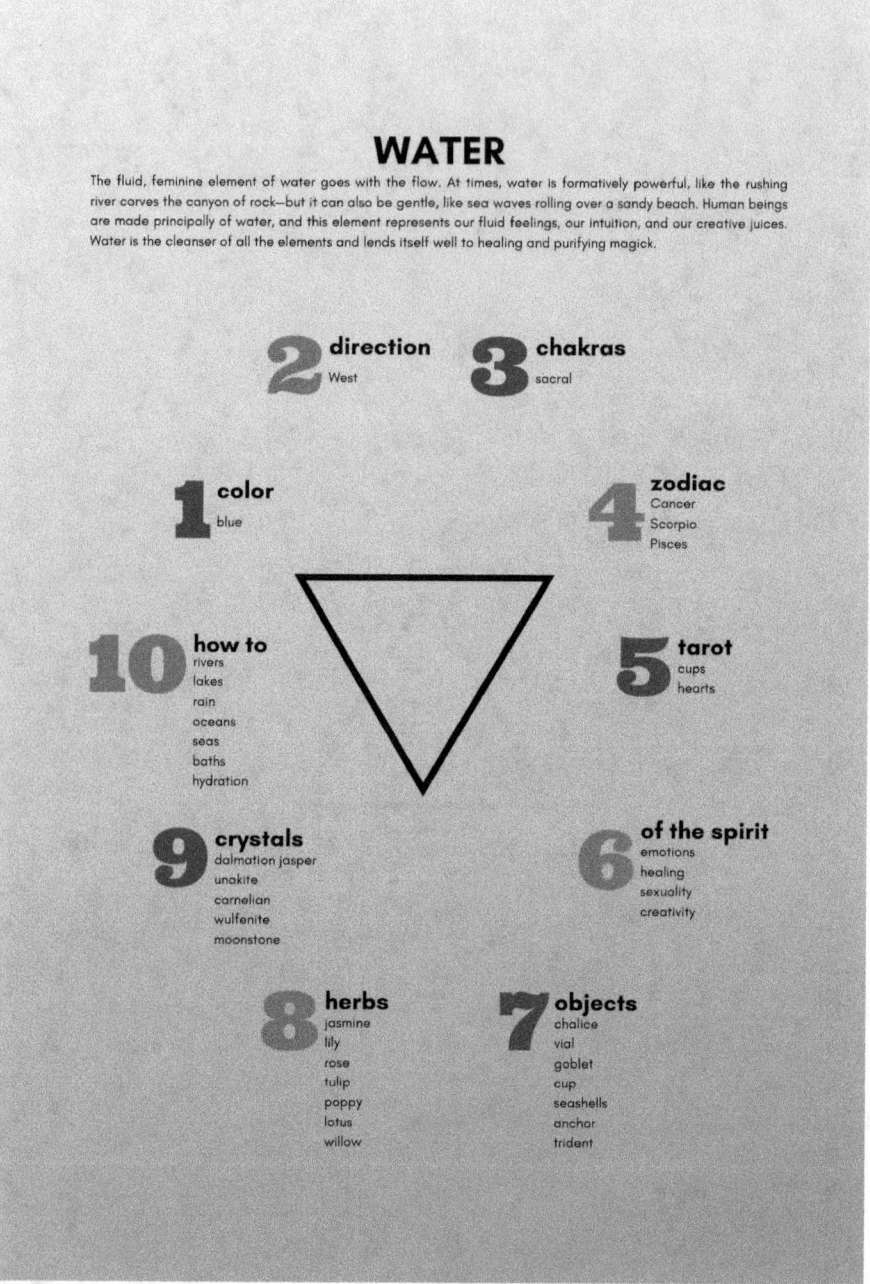

2 direction
West

3 chakras
sacral

1 color
blue

4 zodiac
Cancer
Scorpio
Pisces

10 how to
rivers
lakes
rain
oceans
seas
baths
hydration

5 tarot
cups
hearts

9 crystals
dalmation jasper
unakite
carnelian
wulfenite
moonstone

6 of the spirit
emotions
healing
sexuality
creativity

8 herbs
jasmine
lily
rose
tulip
poppy
lotus
willow

7 objects
chalice
vial
goblet
cup
seashells
anchor
trident

The Phases of the Moon

Mother Moon is a timeless symbol of paganism, earth worship, and witchcraft. The moon represents the divine feminine, the Triple Goddess, while the sun corresponds to the Great Horned God. The moon, in her resplendent glow, holds power over each of us and our lives, as witnessed in the ebb and flow of tides and a woman's reproductive cycle. The moon, as its energy pulls on the water in our bodies, represents our subconscious, our inner world, and a world we navigate with intuition. *This* is why the moon means so much to us witches.

Each month, the Maiden is born and blossoms into her prime during the waxing moon. She grows into the Mother in the light of the full moon, and finally matures into the Crone while the moon's glow wanes. So, as the lunar cycle advances, the moon's energy shifts accordingly. By timing our spells and rituals, witches can make use of Mother Moon's gifts to amplify our magick.

The moon offers many forms of energy and support for all different types of witches. Because the moon changes through a never-ending and dependable cycle, she gives us stability and strength through every phase of our lives. The moon is especially sacred for the feminine energy, as she is connected directly with the element of water and the ideals of a nurturing and protective Goddess.

The Wheel of the Year

Witches don't just see the divinity innate in our inner nature; we *harness* it. Through our craft, we can tap into the magick of the changing of the seasons, as we tap into the nature within ourselves. The Wheel of the Year, the witch's calendar, harkens back to a time before creature comforts, when the summer harvest was key to surviving the harsh, dark winter.

In the Celtic folk tradition, the turning of the seasons is a story told to us through the allegory of the God and Goddess. The Great Horned God rises as a Holy King to rule the darker half of the year, ceding the crown to become the Oak King, his lighter half in the months of light and warmth; meanwhile, the Goddess grows from Maiden to Mother and finally Crone as nature blooms, fruits, and decays. When we witches observe the Wheel of the Year, eternally turning, we tap directly into the spirits of our ancestors and work in harmony with the cycle of the cosmos around us. We invite ourselves to take pause and appreciate the changes in our lives along with the seasons, and in turn, the seasons lend their particular powers to make potent our well-timed spells and magick.

The witch's calendar is marked by the celebrations of eight holy days called sabbats, beginning with Samhain, the witch's new year. There are four greater sabbats—based on pre-Christian fire festivals in Europe—and four lesser sabbats—marking the solstices and equinoxes of the solar calendar.

The lesser sabbats represent transition points between the seasons (e.g., Yule marks the beginning of winter in the northern hemisphere). The greater sabbats were historically celebrated on the nearest full moon to the midpoint between each lesser sabbat, and these festivals celebrate the height of each season's energy (e.g., Samhain, the witch's new year, is in the middle of autumn, when the veil between the worlds is thin).

A Witch's Powers

It is the responsibility of a witch to understand the laws of cause and effect. If mistakes happen, she should remember her intent behind her actions. She should know that a lesser law is washed away by a greater law, and as such, witchcraft is founded on learning to transmute our energies from virtue over vices. The power that comes with witchcraft is an ancient one that has the potential to change lives. And with this power, we must take great care of our actions.

Because nature is a cyclical creature, and she governs the energies throughout the universe, all of the energy that exists now has always been and will always be. When we perform a spell or magick, and we ask the Deities to grant us the power to bring our intentions to fruition, we are committing our energies to the people and spirits involved within the spells we are casting as well as the order of the cosmos. This means that when we act in the auspices of severity, we should be just and righteous. When we act in the auspices of mercy, we should be forgiving and patient. To be harmonious requires our ability to be decisive, and so we must act with both severity and mercy in mind.

Manifestation and Intention

The act of manifestation is not absurd in concept. When magickal powers of the psyche are revealed, the witch may use her clairvoyance to see and predict future events. Think of a Seer with a crystal ball who predicts a flood and warns of holes in boats, among many other things. Witches of today, with such visions are hoped to be able to prevent certain calamities, even through clumsiness. We do this with manifestation, using our powers to make everything we want to experience a reality. It's very simple to use our thoughts, actions, beliefs and emotions, but we go further to manipulate the elements with the help of the Gods and Goddess who rule them. With every spell, we set a clear intention, either mentally, audibly, or by writing it down, and we exercise our veneration for the Deities in equal parts admiration and respect. Prayer is often helpful, but we should also remark on the visions we receive through our third eye, since this is where our intuition sits.

Think of how many times you've prayed next to a candle, or witnessed someone offer incense to a Master or Mistress? Or, how often we have seen different colors of flowers used for certain events, all of which are performed while asking God to look over the people in attendance. These basics to crafting a spell in witchcraft and performing it at home with the family is a very wholesome way to connect to the greater energies throughout the universe.

As we connect with our deities of higher dimensions, we are able to manifest the things that we hope to make true through practical action and measured results. Let's say, for example, that you were hoping to earn the favor of a stranger for cooperation in the affairs of gathering fruit at an orchard. A witch cannot manipulate the thoughts of another, that is black magick; instead, she can make an example of her own free will by picking up fruit and charming the stranger with persuasion to earn the trust and commitment to offer mutual benefit in her cause.

When performing a spell, it is important that you stay focused and clear-minded so that you can speak and feel your intentions fully and pure heartedly. When you have clear and good intentions in what you are doing, it is much more likely that your manifestations will come true without hesitation. To avoid such hesitation, we should be guided by our intuition.

A Witch's Intuition

The intuition of a witch is a very powerful thing. Intuition is how we know something without having to be told. We have a deeper understanding because we are connected to the energies around us and within us, and we don't need explanations or clues to figure out what is happening in our intimate life. The intuition guides us and directs us towards solutions to our problems like a small subtle voice of an angel, and it helps us open doors when we feel like everything else has been closed away. When the howling winds of desire are pushing negative thoughts here and there within our mind, fret not, our intuition will not abandon us as a firm mast to hold our sails upright. Like a beacon, the intuition warns of danger and is not to be ignored, since its subtle indications will save hungry bellies from going underfed, vulnerable children from getting lost at night, and direct us away from dark back alleys full of risks.

Many witches are deeply intuitive and their intuition spans not only the material world, but also the spiritual realm. Intuition can help a witch connect with the great Genies hidden in the ultra dimensions who respond to the language of emotional intelligence. The third-eye chakra is known for its association with higher intelligence and intuition. The third eye manages the screen of the mind, but of course, the crown, or top of the head, is where our etheric body exits when we fall asleep. Deities who guide our etheric body through the needle-sized door at the top of the head do so with perfection and divine grace. Many spells exist to project into the astral dimension, where witches perform the spell work they learn in their grimoire. These dreams must be remembered as the Genies grant us wishes if we intuitively understand their instructions. Spells should be handled with intuitive accuracy and complete veneration for the Gods and Goddesses who supervise the work.

Now that you understand a little more about where witchcraft came from, as well as what it means to modern witches in today's world, we can continue our journey toward spell casting. In the following chapter, we will look at the foundations needed in order to practice magick successfully. Everything from casting a circle to invoking certain energies. We're about to get into the fun stuff now as we dive into the reality of what a life as a witch truly entails.

Chapter 2

The Foundations of Witchcraft Magick

"An altar is a great way to pray and communicate with the Masters and Mistresses of the spiritual realms. It is a nice, dedicated space for you to put together your spell jars and sachets, potions and tinctures, so that you can arrange or disarrange your rituals as you see fit."

Everyone wants a little bit of magick to make their lives easier and better. What most people don't realize is that there is magick to be had right here in our beautiful and natural world. Magick is simply the act of using the energies that link us together with nature to reinforce our intentions. Not every witch wishes to have powers to manipulate the elements, but eventually, every witch realizes she must do so to achieve success in her endeavors. When she does, she brings forth her manifestations and allows us to create real change in our everyday lives.

We can bring change into matters of love and affection with candle spells, using sweetness and soft melodies. We can find wealth in our business with jar spells using bay leaves and black salt. Do you desire the clarity of mind to learn something new? Cast a crystal grid with divine mathematical order and chant ohm. Seeking health after sickness, find your athame and admire the fires in your life, invoke Deities for each one. When we feel vulnerable, find moonwater in the morning and begin to banish or cleanse your spirits until just before noon with three times frankincense smoke throughout the house.

Embracing What Nature has to Offer

Being an intuitive witch starts by incorporating nature as a magickal part of life–it is welcome into our homes and should be part of our daily routines. Becoming one with nature allows us to feel the energies that coincide with the seasons and the animals of nature, too. Learning to live as bears do, hibernating, or owls do, hunting at night, allows us to connect with nature's wisdom. These cyclical routines of nature give us a deeper understanding of the primordial energies that encompass the world. Simply being aware of the moon's cycles and how plants are growing outside can bring us closer to the harmony that we need in order to begin to connect to the woodland Nymphs and water Naiads.

These minor Deities play an enormous role as they organize the cutlery in drawers, handle the glasses in cupboards, and remind us to lock the doors and set the alarm. Having prayed to them and offered colors which enlighten their minds, we can rest knowing they will play with the elementals inside the plants. The elementals are the conscious beings that offer us their biological and chemical attributes to assist us in our spells, potions, oils, tinctures, and balms. Whosoever discovers this given elemental who lives in the pink rose, can summon her quickly with the incantation, *"patch my heart, now let's start."*

Enlisting the Bounties of Nature

Everything that a witch uses in her routines, magick, and spell work comes from nature. Our items are not manmade, unless you consider the ones we make ourselves from nature's bounties. For example, using a rose quartz crystal necklace while you meditate is something manmade; however, it utilizes something that nature has gifted to us.

We, as witches, like to go out and forage and find things that connect with our own energies, things that we are drawn to that have purpose and meaning in what we are trying to accomplish. We may seek out certain flowers and herbs; we might also look for fallen antlers or specific rocks. These items can be used to craft and cast a spell, only making it stronger alongside a witch's own words and intentions.

Everything throughout nature has a certain purpose and meaning behind it. But it is our inner nature where we are bestowed with specific sensory faculties beyond the normal five: see, touch, taste, hear, and feel. Knowing our psychological makeup means that we can use items from nature to help alleviate stress and anxiety or offer success and wealth. Because of how the earth has created gemstones with unique vibrations, plants with bitter flavors, and animals with intelligent behaviors, we can bestow ourselves with such gifts by accessing the beauty of their energies.

Think about how some plants have to struggle to survive out in rocky deserts. These plants work meticulously in order to conserve their water consumption and last in the blistering heat of the day. Then we have the eagle with an eyesight that can target its prey from a mile in the sky. And whales who sing to each other under the ocean floor describing where the best krill are. Like bumblebee dancing in the hive to tell where the nectar and best flower orchard are, mote it be original to you as you feel bestowed by the nature you co-exist with.

The Witch's Grimoire

One very essential tool that every witch should carry is her grimoire. In addition to the things that she is connected with, such as specific sabbats or Deities, this notebook will also contain spell and other things that the witch has created. Some grimoires are handed down through families, generation after generation, as new witches add to the grimoires or use the material as a reference for their own work.

A grimoire does not have to be fancy or perfect. On the contrary, it is best if it is raw and rough and expressive. It is a symbol of your journey and everything you have overcome as you embrace magick and nature in your own practice.

There are also wonderful resources that a witch can utilize in building her grimoire front to back. These include resources like this book of spells, as well as reference books available in libraries and bookstores. Creating your witchcraft magick spell practice will take time. With understanding and patience, you have to be willing to improve from the mistakes you make along the way. *Cast your spells, many upon many, with intention and tells, to feel enabled aplenty.*

Advanced Tools for Frequent Practice

Some witches take their practice a step further and bring their magick into every aspect of their lives and homes. These witches set up dedicated altars somewhere in their living space so that they can conduct spells at ease, or even with others, in a coven. While neither altars nor covens are necessary at all, solitary witches like me can simply go outside and celebrate our magick beneath the light of the moon with nothing more than our words. It is a nice addition once you are comfortable in your practice to join a coven as I did, as you may want to incorporate magick with others too.

An altar is a great way to pray and communicate with the Masters and Mistresses of the spiritual realms. It is a nice, dedicated space for you to put together your spell jars and sachets, potions and tinctures, so that you can arrange or disarrange your magick as you see fit. An altar allows you to cast a spell over weeks, months, and even years. It does not need to be extravagant or even very big; it could be a simple tabletop in the corner of a quiet room, or a box in which secrets are kept hidden. Some witches like to get very creative with their altars, even building entire houses in their honor.

If you choose to create an altar, then having a few essential items will make your magickal practice that much easier. It is wise to have a large dish or plate, preferably something that can withstand heat in case you choose to use fire magick. A pentacle is a mark of protection which is wise to keep on your altar to ward off evil spirits and prying eyes. A small chalice or cup will hold incense and other offerings as it burns and you walk about your space with a finger in the loop. You will utilize it to combine herbs and oils and sometimes even gemstones to create a mixture that can help you with your spells. In addition, small glass jars with corks, cord, and labels are for potions and jar spells. Candleholders, cauldrons, candles, matches, gemstones, mortar and pistle, all yes, yes, yes.

Some experienced witches choose to also keep a wand, an athame, some feathers, animal skin, images of Deities, etc. Your athame could be used to trim an herb, the wand to stir a cauldron, a broom to clean the altar, and pestle to crush egg shells. Pay attention to the colors you are drawn to, and gauge the elaborations to the extent of the temperance of your moods. Simple is often better. Better spells are the way forward.

Witchcraft Magick Throughout the Year

The wheel of the year offers many wonderful opportunities to introduce magick into your life. If you're already familiar with the concepts of magick, then timing your spells to the different sabbats can allow you to practice the aspects of magick with unique results.

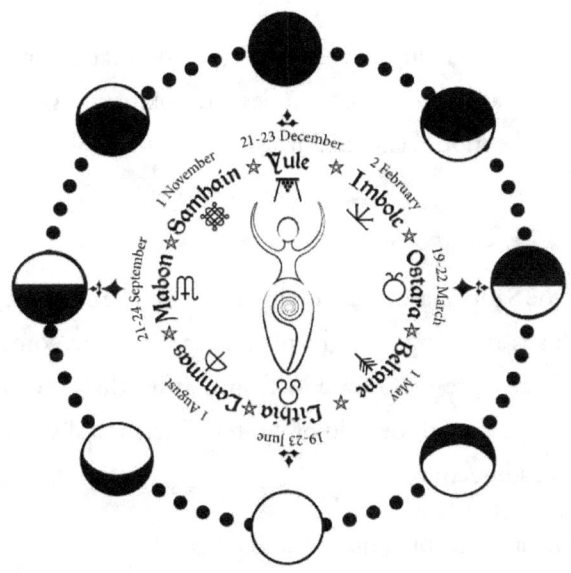

Samhain

This sabbat, on October 31, marks the day when the veil is at its thinnest between our world and the spirit world. We celebrate this day by paying respect to those who have passed on and died. During this time, we use the things from nature that are connected to the end of the cycle as well as the spirit realm.

- Crystals such as bloodstone, obsidian, and onyx

- Candles and items in the colors of black, purple, and orange

- Vegetation such as nuts, pumpkins, patchouli, oak trees, apples, and garlic

- Associated animals like cats, spiders, and bats

- Deities such as Anubis, Cerridwen, Osiris, and Rhiannon

Decorating your living space as well as your altar during this time will involve things such as dark-colored candles, pumpkins and gourds, things that are connected to the moon, and cauldrons.

Yule

During the Sabbat, around December 21, we celebrate the rebirth of the Sun God as this is the longest night of the year, but the coming days grow longer and longer. Here we use items from nature that are connected with rebirth in the darkness and the cold of winter. There is a sliver of hope for the warmth that will soon come.

- Crystals such as ruby, quartz, and emerald

- Candles and items in the colors of red, silver, gold, and green

- Vegetation such as oranges, holly, potatoes, pine, cinnamon, and peppermint

- Associated animals like bears, deer, owls, and geese

- Deities such as Odin, Frau Holle, and the Holly King

Decorating your home and altar during this time will involve items such as lights, bells, wreaths, and nuts. Yule is a time when we try to illuminate the innocent to the frailties of our bodies against the cold, with joyful singing, layers of protection, and loving feasts. It is also the winter solstice, a greater sabbat, and a celestial event, perfect for giving gifts.

Imbolc

This sabbat, held around February 2nd, is a fire festival celebrating the warming of the earth. This new warmth that is bringing a bit of life into the world comes directly between Yule and Ostara. At this time, we focus on the awaking natural world as our home begins to stir with liveliness.

- Crystals such as rose quartz, aventurine, and amethyst

- Candles and other items in the colors of pastel green, pink, and white

- Vegetation such as birch trees, lemons, poppy seeds, lavender, and honey

- Associated animals like sheep, lamb, and groundhogs

- Deities like Eros, Pan, and Brigid

During this time, we will decorate our homes and altars with things that are representative of a newness in nature. These things may include sun wheels, fresh flower petals, and Brigid's cross.

Ostara

This Sabbat, held around March 21st, marks the first day of spring. Here, on this Spring Equinox, we are celebrating the brand new warmth as the forces of light and dark come into balance. The days are increasingly longer and warmer, and it is a time to focus on fertility and abundance.

- Crystals such as aquamarine and moss agate

- Candles and other items in the colors of blue, yellow, and green

- Vegetation such as cherries, spinach, lilac, jasmine, and cedar

- Associated animals like chickens, butterflies, and rabbits

- Deities such as Freya, Eostre, and Cybele

This time is closely associated with Easter, a Christian holiday that has pulled many ancient Pagan constructs into its modern rituals. We decorate our homes and altars with clovers, baskets filled with eggs, fresh budding branches, and pastel ribbons.

Beltane

This sabbat, typically held around May 1st, is another fire festival that marks the distance between two greater sabbats. On this day, we celebrate the height of spring as the world is fully alive and growing. There's abundant light and warmth to enjoy and embrace.

- Crystals such as citrine, fluorite, and diamond

- Candles and other items in the colors of bright green, yellow, blue, and purple

- Vegetation such as roses, strawberries, birch trees, and stone fruits

- Associated animals like frogs, goats, and bees

- Deities like Artemis, Hera, and Dionysus

To decorate our homes and altars during this time, we utilize flower blossoms and floral crowns, maypoles, mixtures of herbs, and symbols of the animals that are prevalent during this lively time.

Litha

This Sabbath is celebrated around June 21st, and it is the summer solstice, a time when the light is longest before our days begin to shrink. Here we celebrate the last liveliness of the year as the Oak King returns to bring darkness to our world. We use items in our rituals that are associated with vigor, strength, and power.

- Crystals such as jade, lapis lazuli, and tiger's eye
- Candles and other items in the colors of red, gold, green, and yellow
- Vegetation such as lemons, berries, tomatoes, basil, and thyme
- Associated animals like crustaceans, snakes, fish, and dragons
- Deities like Juno, Apollo, Hesta, and Ra

On this day, we decorate our homes and altars with abundant fresh fruits and other crops that are currently ripe. We also use seashells and other symbols of oceanic life, as well as mirrors to help us gain reflection on the abundance we've already received.

Lammas

This sabbat is typically held around August 1st, and it is a fire festival that sits directly between the summer solstice and the autumn equinox. This is a time when we celebrate our first and earliest harvest, thanking Mother Earth for all the wonderful things we've received during the warmer months. We utilize the things in nature that are currently abundant and prevalent.

- Crystals such as topaz, peridot, and carnelian

- Candles and other items in the colors of bronze, golden yellow, and dark orange

- Vegetation such as rosemary, sycamore trees, corn, grapes, and nuts

- Associated animals like the stag, crows, and the robin

- Deities like Persephone, Demeter, Isis, and Lugh

Lammas is also known as Lughnasadh due to the connection with the God Lugh. On this day, we decorate our homes and our altars with cornucopias, fall flowers, sunflowers, and corn dolls. This is just the beginning of the cooler days in the wheel of the year, as we begin to embrace the darkness and the deeper shades that nature offers.

Mabon

The Sabbath is the final one in the wheel of the year, and it is also the autumn equinox, typically celebrated around September 21st. On this day, we recognize how the balance between light and dark is once again equal, and that the coming days will bring more darkness and cooler nights.

- Crystals such as sapphire, tourmaline, and cat's eye

- Candles and other items in the colors of brown, deep red, and dark green

- Vegetation such as warm spices, walnuts, gourds, and onions

- Associated animals like the hawk, squirrels, and eagles

- Deities like Mabon, Fortuna, and Concordia

During this time, we decorate our homes and altars with dark flowers that are abundant in nature. We also use nuts and seeds, as well as corn and mums. This is the second harvest festival of the year, marking a time when we celebrate all that earth has provided for us during the wonderful and lengthy warmth.

Sabbat Practice

During each sabat, as well as before and after, the observances of the seasons will be your guiding reminders of the changes taking place. Don't forget to combine your knowledge of nature with the knowledge of yourself. As the Triple Goddess is at her most fertile, her magick will harvest with equal creative power. When indications of her cycle are complete, her balance in waiting for the new moon to form will be her greatest asset. The reliance on the Horned God to provide through the winter as a spirit, before his rebirth in the spring, is essential to feel protected, just as is his duty to plant and work the soil in the summer months.

Witchcraft Magick Spells

Chapter 3

The Psychology and Philosophy of Witchcraft

"Initiation into these higher realms is performed through the etheric dream dimension in the sleeping state of the practicing witch. "

Witchcraft takes us on a journey throughout our lives, touching on every aspect of who we are and what we strive to accomplish. It creates a web of knowledge and comfort as we go from one sphere to the next on the tree of life, and one sabbat to the next on the wheel of the year. Throughout this journey, we learn more about our place in the vast universe as we begin to understand all of the things that work together to create life and enjoy our existence.

As witches, we are to know and understand the underpinnings of nature and the divine spiritual kingdom within it. What is commonly misunderstood is how we experience the afterlife. If it wer possible to die and resurrect, wouldn't it have already been marketed as fundamentally profitable at an online store? Certainly, it would. Anyone drawn to afterlife concepts is not particularly foolish nor impractical. However, I am not talking about mere snake oil! In fact, there are practical aspects of the secrecy about afterlife realities I should reveal. The resurrection of souls after death is a deeply psychological, occult reality. I refer to the resurrection of the spirit like the Great Horned God. Our plain-clothed physical body is governed by the laws of the physical dimension (3rd), but the etheric body (4th), astral and mental bodies (5th), well they are governed by the causal realities (6th)! These bodies live on after the physical body perishes, only to be born again to return to influence the world by paying more karma and doing more good deeds. Initiated into the secret path, our divine will (7th, or zero dimension) shines with splendor!

Astrology and the Zodiac

Because we are children of the stars, we have a constitution similar to the macrocosmos, where laws of physics apply similarly to the microcosmos inside of us. This astrological makeup within all of us comes from being born beneath constellations that have provided us with energy and purpose. We are not destined to live a specific life where we have no choice, but we can find comfort in knowing that we are part of a collective that works together in harmony.

Elemental Symbology

Just as everything else within nature and witchcraft is associated with elements, so are the signs of the Zodiac. There are four distinct groupings of signs: fire, earth, air, and water.

Fire signs, those of Aries, Leo, and Sagittarius, are known to be courageous and enthusiastic. As much as fire can consume and destroy, so can it create. Fire signs embrace this fully, stepping out into the light and taking praise for their accomplishments. Excited and extroverted, the fire signs are always adventuring as they seek new and interesting experiences.

Earth signs, which include Taurus, Virgo, and Capricorn, are practical by nature. These signs have a good sense of worth and are connected to the physical world in ways that the other signs are not. Earth is a symbol of physical health and material wealth, both of which the earth signs are well versed in. They are steady workers focused on the end goal, and their strength and discipline gives them purpose.

Air signs are the Geminis, Libras, and Aquarians! They enjoy conversation as much as truth and justice. These signs are great at communication, and they also act as intermediaries during debates. The air element is also one of new ideas, and these signs embrace an awareness for innovation that is both enlightening and necessary in the world. Air signs do not only speak their truth, they try to understand themselves as much as others in the pursuit of a better future.

Water signs are Cancer, Scorpio, and Pisces, who are nurturing and open-minded. Water signs are persuaded by not only what is seen, but also by what is unseen. Water signs are intuitive and are able to understand people on a deeper level. They naturally balance between emotions and intellect, weighing every situation with both their heart and their mind.

Lunar Phases

The moon is a magickal and whimsical satellite in the skies overhead. Set as a measurement of patience, she moves gracefully across the sky, shining brightly in the dark until she disappears. The moon is actually the daughter of the Earth, and although it's not visible to the physical eye, because she exists in the spirit world, Lilith is a daughter of the moon, orbiting her like a satellite. Lilith is the famed Deity who was the first wife of Adam of the Bible.

The phases of the moon play a role in the energies that we feel and receive from her every month. It is already well known that the moon sways the tides, connecting deep with the waters of the Earth. Like the waters of our body, we are especially tied to the phases of the moon, as each female on the earth also has her phases. Our moon signs, as opposed to our sun signs, are determined by the location of the moon at the moment of our birth. Moon signs rule our emotions, our feelings, intuition, and memories. For example, a Pisces moon sign may have mysterious healing powers because of their smooth personality and presence, like the moon in the sky.

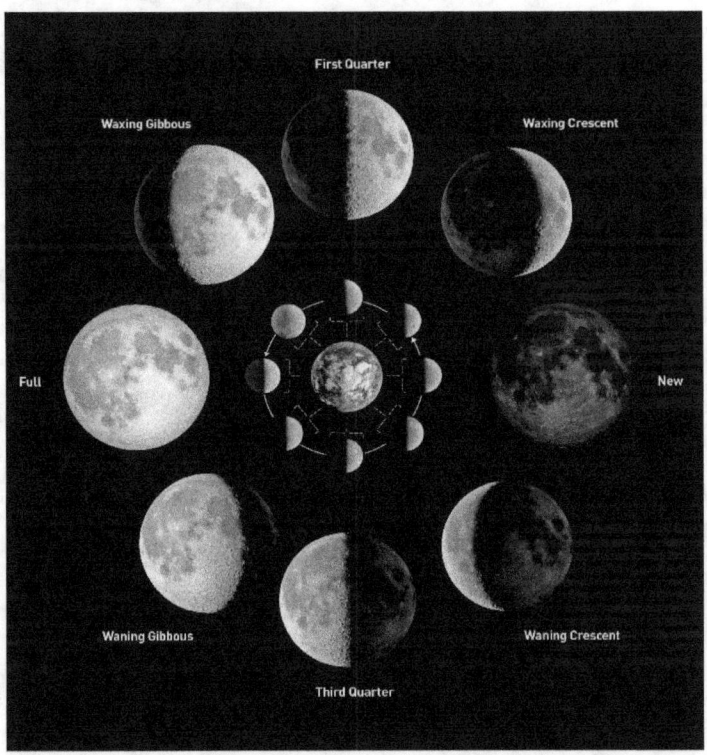

The New Moon

This is a time for new beginnings. The new moon represents a brand new sense of life and energy. This is when we can begin planting the seeds for a new spell that we may bring to fruition during the full moon. Our intentions with each spell take this journey of the moon's cycle. The new moon is our fresh start; a moment of initiation when we are emerging from the darkness and heading toward the light.

The Waxing Crescent Moon

The waxing Crescent moon is the first sliver of light that is emerging as the new moon gains more energy. This is a time to nurture those intentions you have planted as seeds sown for the new beginnings you were hoping to achieve. We are taking special care at this time to focus on the details that will help us bring our intentions to light near the full moon.

The First Quarter Moon

During the first quarter moon, we are starting to gain momentum as our initial seeds of intention begin to take hold in the real world. Roots have dug in, and activity has been set in motion, and everything that we are working towards is beginning to find a firm grasp in our lives. Tempted to dig up roots, we might spoil our intentions unless we dominate the waters of creation. When we focus on pouring our energy into organized ideas, we maintain the mystery of our ways and rise up to flourish.

The Waxing Gibbous Moon

During this phase, we take a moment to reflect on how things have begun to grow. We remember our patience as we realize the spells set may turn out better than expected. The full moon is fast approaching, and that is the time when our spells have the greatest potential to come to full effect. Here in the waxing gibbous moon, however, we take a moment to pause. We must be clear-minded and pure of heart before we head into the most energetic moment of the moon phases. This is a time for meditation as we allow our inner spirit to absorb the nurturing energies of the emerging full moon.

The Full Moon

Under the light of the full moon, we celebrate the shining and illuminating Triple Goddess in all her glory. This is a time when the moon has the most energy throughout her cycles, and we must be grateful and show our gratitude for all the protection and nurturing that she offers to us. This is a time to celebrate life and feminine energy as we make positive use of these bold moments. Many spells are cast during the full moon, come through at the full moon, and are even taught at the full moon.

The Waning Gibbous Moon

We have passed the peak of maximum energy for the full moon, and now we are beginning to wane. At this time, we release the energies we have accumulated from when we were performing our spells and magick. We let go and have faith that the cycle will come around again–although next time with different intentions. During the waning, we value the concept of the conception, in that we have reaped the fruits from our seeds of intention and now we can share in the abundance of what we have sowed. Here we can also look to others to form companionship.

The Last Quarter Moon

In the same way that the first quarter moon was about rooting your seeds of intention into reality, the last quarter moon is about removing those roots and allowing the plants to decompose. The monthly harvest of intentions has fulminated, and now we are entering a time of transition. The energies of the full moon are still residual, giving us a bit of warmth and light as we look toward the darkness ahead. Here we are thankful for the graces we have been gifted, and we use this appreciation to praise others.

The Waning Crescent Moon

During the waning Crescent moon, we are faced with the nearing darkness. Now is the time that we surrender ourselves to the cycle and allow for the new moon to come and provide us with new beginnings once again. At this time, we reflect on the entire cycle and everything that we have created and brought to fruition. We take time to understand whether we made the right choices and how we can do better as the cycle begins again. This is a perfect time to find rest and allow your personal energies to heal and restore from the inside out.

The Cycle Continues

As the new moon arrives again, we have put everything of the past cycle behind us, and we can now move forward with another new beginning. This endless and dependable cycle gives us strength and perseverance as we know that the moon will grant us the energy we need to bring forth even our most difficult intentions. Throughout the month, we have worked on something dear to us, planting the seeds of our magick to create change. After reaping the fruits of our laborers, we have enjoyed the harvest and been grateful for everything the moon has granted. After a brief rest in the dim light of the ending cycle, the darkness finally arrives and clears away everything so that we can begin anew.

Types of Witches

Everything in magick is closely intertwined. Some witches feel drawn toward specific items and magick, and their practice will vary based on how they want to incorporate these items. Throughout the world of witchcraft, there are diverse ways to practice magick. These different types of magick are not set ways that a witch must conform. The beauty of witchcraft is that we can take what we enjoy putting our intuition to good use however we feel best. Some witches may feel very comfortable within a certain type of magick, and others will blend the lines as they find their own paths in life.

Kitchen Witch

Magick that revolves around the kitchen is all about cooking meals and providing nutrition for yourself and loved ones. A kitchen witch is someone who enjoys the fire of the hearth and can comfortably dance around the flames of passion. She uses fresh and wild vegetation for her specific purposes. Through food and drinks, a kitchen witch will mix in sigils to her decor, and whisper mantras as she combines special herbs to enhance her intentions. Chapter 7 is of particular importance to the kitchen witch.

Elemental Witch

A witch who practices elemental magick will incorporate all four elements deliberately into everything she does in order to seal her work with the pentagram. She will rely heavily on earth, air, fire, and water in order to feel the ether of the environment. Elemental witches are naturally empaths and use the elements to protect others as well as themselves. Her spells require interpreting numbers and the Tarot while offering predictions of certainty. She feels comfortable reading auras of the etheric body that the uninitiated have not begun to see.

Cosmic Witch

A witch who uses cosmic magick will focus her spells and energy specifically on lunar phases, meteor showers, the wheel of the year, and all other celestial objects. This witch will use celestial events to her benefit, emphasizing her intentions with raw, macrocosmic and microcosmic universalities and a high level of intuition. She studies birth charts and moon signs, and enjoys protecting the vulnerable.

Grey Witch

A grey witch is someone who practices magick in a neutral setting and is not entirely confident in there not being a need for hostile spells. Some witches believe that the concept of black magick doesn't exist, which it certainly does, and so grey witches sit between white and black magick. A grey witch is known to be a Mistress of vagueness, and avoids ethical questions in order to let others decide for themselves. She balances what is needed from magick with what humanity requires. She is a protector and will use her magick to disarm her opponents and unmask traitors.

Green Witch

A green witch will embrace all that nature has to offer in loving abundance. She will incorporate plants, mushrooms, and components of trees as she crafts spells and tries to observe the signs of nature. This type of witch spends plenty of time in her garden, learning all there is about the elementals that she incorporates in her spells. The witch is excellent at crafting medicinal tinctures and balms that can heal in a pure way as nature has intended. She uses clairaudience to see and work with salamanders (fire), sylphs (water), undines (air) and gnomes (earth).

Divination Witch

A witch who is involved with divination magick will spend her time communicating with the Gods and Goddesses. This witch is known to delve in the arts of the tarot, as well as other divination techniques, like bone magick, palm reading, etc. Those who are naturally drawn toward psychic tendencies are great at preparing horoscopes and blessing a new home or altar (divining). These witches are generally well guarded and focus quite a bit on intelligence and protection spells.

Traditional Witch

A witch who practices traditional witchcraft is one who uses the old ways that came before Gardnerian Wicca. These witches are often hereditary, in that they learned their practice from elder family members. Quite often, traditional witches will also be solitary witches, practicing their magick on their own as opposed to within a coven. A lot of principles that are infused with Wicca come from ancient practices, but there are some that Gardener did not include or altered a little for the more modern world. Traditional witches focus their practice on anthropology, the study of the human being and how she evolves through time but still stays the same. She communicates well with Masons, Knights Templars, and other Elders.

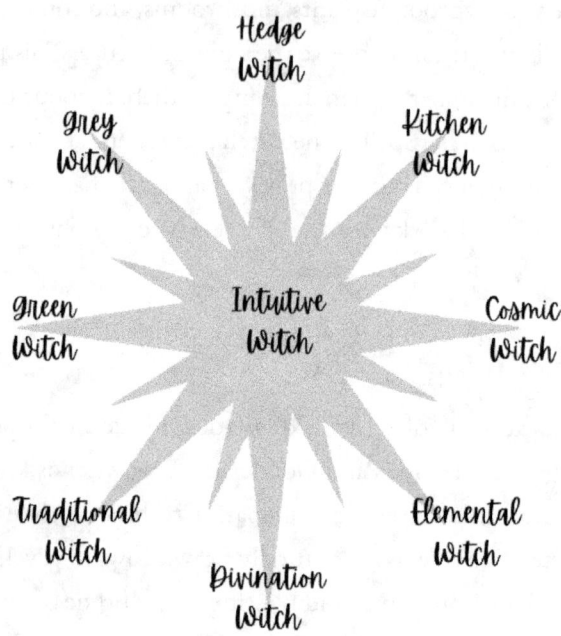

Solar Magick

Countless magickal forms exist across the globe, but there is one common thread amongst all witches. These are the solar robes and garments which a witch dresses with to represent her advancement in witchcraft. In fact, a stitch witch is one who enjoys sewing together fabrics with needle and thread. Stitch witches like to crochet or knit, creating items for people who have been initiated into higher realms on the tree of life. As ordained by the Deities of the spiritual world, it's clear to see the award of crowns and headdresses for spiritual exaltations and intelligence, masks and blindfolds for tests of comprehension, robes and jackets for love and abundance, belts for protection, necklaces and rings for wealth, wrist bands and armbands representing health, pants and skirts signifying the mystery of sex, while shoes, boots, or sandals symbolize control over instincts and sincerity of intention. Initiation into these higher realms is performed through the etheric dream dimension in the sleeping state of the practicing witch.

Since witchcraft is an occult practice, a life-long affair should be formed within the individual witch to devote herself only to what she is initiated. Exploring the various avenues of witchcraft, therefore, depends on the temperament of the witch and how she is led by the merits of her heart. The occult faculties of clairaudience and clairvoyance allow any witch to hear beyond and see beyond the mere physical planes into the spiritual realms, now known as etheric planes and above. These are deeply personal psychological advancements and should be regarded intuitively, especially among other witches. We witches all recognize the fervor and excitement about achieving higher powers, as is evident through the abundance of #WitchTok posts on TikTok. But we should recognize the importance of welcoming baby witches into the path of witchcraft, as the start of the path of initiation is the most difficult to find. I'm glad you found it with me here.

Life as a Witch

Some people who are new to witchcraft wonder if they are choosing the right path for themselves. Others might have some doubt as to whether spells will truly work for them. Remembering your innocence as a child playing with sticks, while 'boiling' and 'bubbling' stones with leaves and mud in the bathtub should be intuitively understood to be the alchemy we are all capable of. This is the alchemy of the philosophical stone, the magickal stone that when worked with fire and sulfur can turn lead into gold.

Witches are the fortunate few who intuitively understand the alchemy of this magickal metallurgy. The lead represents the animal instincts of aggression and intellectualization or any attempts at mind control. The gold is the innumerable elaborations of the spirit, the divine witch's soul. When the lead of the personality is transformed into the gold of the spirit, we have an illustrious fountain of springing joyful exuberance coursing through our mental sphere of activity. Crowned with emotional purity, the witch who bravely uses her gut instinct or hunch, can act compassionately, spelling out opportunities to not only reach a life of enlightened thought, but also of conscious will.

This path is not for everyone, and those who stray are certain to get lost and drift unwittingly into failure. The witchcraft I have learned I am prepared to teach, and although there are no certifications to be a solitary witch, there are occult tests which few have been able to pass. Earning the right to reveal any measure of the path of witchcraft is a rite of initiation, as the judges of karma test us to help others only. Selfish endeavors will only be met by disappointment and rejection. So I pray that you heed this warning. Only read on if you are prepared to open your heart to alleviate the suffering of humanity. The most experienced witches can enter into lairs of filth and demure, and cast charms to enlighten and invigorate the ill and sick to live again. This is an inward journey, one of great peril, because what exists on the outside, filth, demure, and ugliness so vile you might gag, so, too, exists within. Perform these spells with utmost humility and see your internal world, the occult secret of your inner paradise, flourish and blossom with happiness and inspiration. So mote it be.

PART II

MAGICK

In this portion of the book, we will go more in-depth into the items and practices that are involved in witchcraft. We will discuss everything from preparing spell incantations and meditations to divinations and the use of aromatic herbs. As we spoke before, your own personal type of witchcraft will depend on the passions that you are deciding to get involved with, as well as the lifestyle you want to live. You may be more drawn towards cord-cutting and hexing your ex, than casting a circle of forgiveness and observing the darkness of anticipating a new moon, but I will help you to offer vigilance in this regard, among many others. Really, witchcraft is so much more than the quick confluence of marketing your emotions and justifying them with lunar behaviors. Even though you may choose a very specific path through witchcraft, understanding the different elements that go into magickal practice will help you gain a more complete knowledge over the entire subject.

In this section, you will gain a better understanding of tools to add to your grimoire–the pentacle, sword, cup, and wand. You will learn just how meaningful each tool is for the purpose it provides. This will allow you to not only follow the spells outlined in this book, but you will also develop the confidence you need to create your own spells. Witchcraft is a practice, meaning that we work at it little by little throughout our entire lives. We begin by taking knowledge from those who came before us, learning from their ways as we discover the basics of what it means to be a witch. Along the way, we begin to discover our affinities to certain practices which allow us to do good during this lifetime. We pay karma and lift the veil between the land of the living and the dead. With confidence, and basic knowledge for the items that we will use and their correspondences, we create our own style of witchcraft and embrace it to the fullest. At this point, with our grimoires brimming and our energies aligned, we can begin to create the spells that we wish to use to manifest real change in our own lives from scratch.

Witchcraft Magick Spells

Chapter 4

Family, Kids, and Familiars

"They are especially sensitive to the subtle energies of the spiritual realms before their personalities are formed--experiencing dreams of flying, speaking languages from past lives, and reminding us of what innocence really is."

As witches, our main purpose in life is to be happy with ourselves. We do this by following the path of initiation, that of love and light, while bringing happiness within us to every new opportunity. When it comes to witchcraft and our families, a witch should realize how she came to follow her own path, and beset to let others do the same. Although my husband is also a witch, not all witches are required nor destined to find their family this way.

Instead, a witch should be humble in her own regard for her decisions to practice witchcraft, and invite others to learn more about it! Children are genuinely curious about crystals and herbs, colors and incense, and potions to drink. If they wish to question more, we say to them, *"the fiery solar energy of the sun heats us and drives the photosynthesis of the earth to recycle the air for us to breathe while nourishing us with bountiful food. But, if it weren't for the moon, we would be shunted by darkness at night, preyed on by predators whose minds are not yet tempered by the wisdom of witchcraft."*

Some people wonder whether witchcraft is something we should expose our children to, that it might seem dangerous or taboo. This simply is not the case. Showing children a spiritual life with symbols and sigils in your home is precisely the way to help them connect with spiritual emotions later on as they reach adolescence.

In addition, children pass through the realization of our existence as intellectual animals, and how our ability to harmonize with nature requires us to harmonize with ourselves, otherwise we succumb to our animal instincts. Gaining insight into the intelligence of nature allows us to accept our human condition with humility, learning from the crow to be a trickster, from the squirrel to plan for winter, and the dolphin to enjoy pleasure.

As children are uniquely born with their thymus gland still active, they are especially sensitive to the subtle energies of the spiritual realms before their personalities are formed – experiencing dreams of flying, speaking languages from past lives, and reminding us of what innocence really is. As we remember that by gaining dominion over nature, the four elements, and remarking on our spiritual paths of witchcraft, initiations into higher and higher realms of practice will be presented to us. In this, we are meant to remember our past lives, and communicate with the Gods and Goddesses of ancient times.

Creating Everyday Magick

Just as a God-fearing mother may pray throughout the day and ask the Heavens above to protect her family and help them to grow healthy and happy, a witch will do the same while connecting with her chosen craft. In fact, we aim to act as intuitive witches who utilize the knowledge of our inner nature to harmonize with the energies around us so as to enhance our spiritual connection with the Gods and Goddesses wherever we go. This is a combination of all facets of witchcraft, from kitchen witchery to stitch witchery.

These small things throughout our day add up to become a complete lifestyle, as we ultimately care for the innocence and purity of children while enjoying the beautiful energies of adults. We can use our magick every day, even in the smallest ways, to create positive change for everyone that we love and care about. Little prayers to our most loved Deities can be said on the go as we sprinkle salt to protect our doorways. Sigils can be added to spell jars to personalize a healing spell for yourself or someone else going through troubles. Specific herbs can be tasted, like lemon or honey, to mark a ritual rite of passage from one sphere of advancement on the tree of life, to the next.

A witch's words and her intentions are, again, her most powerful tool. It is her wish to see things come true, and she pours her energy into her purpose with all of her heart. Nothing can hold a witch back when she believes in herself and knows that she is living her life to the fullest from the foundation up to the crown. With her powerful words and her desire to create change, a witch can make anything happen.

Be wary, however, that magick is hard work. It takes dutiful exercise and discipline to bring things to reality. Manifestation is for everyone–a witch must learn careful planning and acquire the knowledge of her ancestors in order to develop the right skills and become a divinely intuitive witch.

Tracy Addams

Witchcraft Magick Spells

Chapter 5

Arcane Wisdom:

Divination and the Magick of the Intuition

"We may be presented a card to read in our dreams by the deities of higher dimensions, and should rely on our knowledge of the Tarot to take intuitive action."

There are all sorts of magickal symbols and icons throughout the natural world that witches will use in their practice. Numbers and symbols are the very fabric of our existence. Without understanding numbers, the witch will lose her battles in the spheres of thought amidst tenacious demons of the mind. We need to quell the mind with the whip of willpower, and deliver angelic poems of emotional perfection. To cast spells properly requires a witch to know how to divine numbers and read symbols.

Numerology

One of the many amazing aspects of nature is how mathematical and rhythmic it can be. The perfection of prisms, spheres, columns, pyramids are modeled by observing nature–within us and without. Numbers within numerology represent perfect measurements from the etheric plane (astral or dream dimension). Messages from the Masters and Mistresses appear as signs for us to interpret.

The number one represents fresh beginnings. Seeing the number one indicates that we are about to be or currently are faced with a new opportunity. The number one is masculine and inspires an initiatory force. Keyword: initiation.

The number two represents balance and unity. Throughout the world there are typically two faces, or two aspects, to the things that Mother Nature has created. The number two is therefore feminine. The number two is also a symbol of a partnership that is either already present in our life or coming our way. Keyword: unity.

The number three represents communion. Communion becomes communication, and by listening, speaking, and praying we develop self-expression, and so all of our creativity is governed by the number three. Because the universe is mental, the number three reminds us to connect with our divine self and embrace crossing the bridge of spirituality with firm ground underfoot. Keyword: communion.

The number four represents foundations. Four is all about the responsibility and dedication you put into your passions and the relationships around you. When we remain devout and work toward a legacy, the number four marks expectations. When in need of order and organization, the number four allows us to embrace rules in life in order to cooperate. Keyword: stability.

The number five signifies change. It represents how we adapt to our changes, as well as the bravery and adventurous spirit that is needed in order to seek out necessary changes. The number five predicts a fall, and we should be wise to descend to the root of issues. Keyword: change.

The number six represents a decision between the path of the virgin or the path of temptation. In the occult path of witchcraft, there are many tests of initiation, and so I advise every witch to use love to pass those tests. The number six directs us to make decisions aligned with our true purpose, our knowledge of self, and confidence to remain independent. Keyword: harmony.

The number seven embodies the ideals of wisdom and knowledge. Not only is this wisdom physical, but it is ultimately emotional, mental and causal. Any witch will confirm when she has been instructed in the astral planes by the Deities she worships. The number seven is also representative of justice and logic. Keyword: strategy.

The number eight represents abundance beyond measurement. With the number eight, we can synchronize into harmony with nature as our friend. Intimacy is ruled by number eight, as well as wealth. The infinity sign reminds us how eight can either overwhelm or allow us to rejoice in resplendency. Keyword: evolution.

The number nine represents the creative energies at the base of the tree of life—our sexual energies. When we balance properly between masculine and feminine energies, our creative forces can be used to emblazon our psychic faculties with love and light. The number nine inspires health, where the microcosmic forces within our blood also are at war to fight illness and promote life. Keyword, creativity.

The number ten is the number of alchemy. It is the epiphany of entirety, representing the key of perpetual motion. It reminds us that although we do not pray to the personality, it is indeed necessary. The number ten is practical magick in action. When knowledge and learned experience are brewing, we have the number ten. Keyword: fulfillment.

Numerology continues on and into the infinite. Multiples of 100 signify initiation into major mysteries. We handle numbers intuitively, by adding them when they are presented to us. The number 27 is therefore $2 + 7 = 9$, a minor initiation into the crucible of creation. Again, 119, a major initiation, is $1 + 1 + 9 = 11$, which is $1 + 1 = 2$, divine feminine. When the tarot is combined with numbers, we learn of the major arcana, going from zero to 21. These are also divinely used with the study of numbers, but also contain the relevance of the elements related to spell casting, and imagery, to guide the intuition through struggle and onto spiritual fulfillment. Remember, this too shall pass.

Tarot

The Tarot, a Bohemian word, is a widely popular divination tool used by witches to discern how circumstances and events can be resolved with the lightning accuracy of the intuitive power of the heart. Any nervousness or anxiety surrounding the use of the tarot comes from the fear of the unknown, and the common misconception that the Tarot will provide you with bad news or a future that would be devastating. Tarot is actually only providing us messages that are presently important and can help us make better decisions for ourselves and those we care most about. Reading the Tarot is not necessarily telling the future, it is merely predicting. The experienced witch understands the wisdom of combining opportunity with right action.

The difference between knowing the Tarot and not knowing is through the process of initiation. By learning and practicing, anyone can develop the skill, but persuading someone to believe what they learn depends on the depth of faith they have in their intuition. The Tarot is haughtily misinterpreted by the intellect of the mind. Managing the massive intellect as a feather weighed against the merits of the heart is the measure of Maat from the *Book of the Dead*. Such imagery illustrates succinctly the frame of mind necessary to feel prepared and capable of intuitively interpreting someone's life with a spread of cards. It is indeed the way of the witch to do so.

The Major Arcana

The Major Arcana holds 22 cards numbered zero through 21. These cards are not connected to the elements like the Minor Arcana are, and they each hold a specific importance for the reading. Some people like to do readings with only the Major Arcana to get a quick message while invoking the assistance of a God or Goddess.

0/The Fool: Innocence, Foolishness, and Recklessness

1/The Magician: Adaptation, Creation, and Deception

2/The High Priestess: Intuition, Unconsciousness, and Repression

3/The Empress: Beauty, Luxury, and Selfishness

4/The Emperor: Structure, Rationality, and Domination

5/The Hierophant: Legacy, Servitude, and Tradition

6/The Lovers: Unity, Indecision, and Conflict

7/The Chariot: Discipline, Accomplishment, and Purposelessness

8/Strength: Courage, Conviction, and Cowardice

9/The Hermit: Solitude, Awareness, and Loneliness

10/The Wheel: Fate, Fortune, and Waywardness

11/Persuasion: Truth, Fairness, and Dishonesty

12/The Apostolate: Sacrifice, Release, and Fear

13/Immortality: Metamorphosis, Change, and Death

14/Temperance: Patience, Discovery, and Disharmony

15/Passion: Pleasure, Materialism, and Freedom

16/The Tower: Fragility, Turmoil, and Prevention

17/Hope: Protection, Restoration, and Discouragement

18/Twilight: The Moon, Intuition, and Confusion

19/Inspiration: The Sun, Celebration, and Depression

20/Resurrection: Judgment, Awakening, and Apathy

21/Transmutation: The World, Completion, and Emptiness

The Minor Arcana

The 56 Minor Arcana are one part of the classic 78-card Tarot deck. They consist of pip cards, which are all of the numbered cards including the ace. Then we have the court cards, which are Pages, Knights, Queens, and Kings. The Minor Arcana can be read by using a standard playing card deck just by replacing the ace with one, the Kings and Queen respectively remain the same, and the Page and Knight take on one personality in the Jack. Some people like to use standard playing cards because of their size and convenience. If used for witchcraft, the traditional suits are seen as Hearts/Cups, Clubs/Wands, Spades/Swords and Diamonds/Pentacles.

  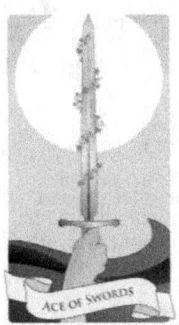 

The intuitive way to read the Minor Arcana is to reduce them to their four aces, and align the element within the suit to draw a conclusion. The suits in the Minor Arcana represent each of the four elements. The suit of Pentacles is connected to air, Cups is connected to water, Swords is connected to fire, and Wands is connected to Earth. We can use what we know about each element to guide us in understanding what these suits will mean when they show up in a reading.

When we find the ten of Swords upright, we have the Major Arcana ten, alchemy, organized by the fire of comprehension, through swords. Our ability to actualize our efforts to achieve victory of the spirit over the personality revives our faith in continued spell work.

Again, the six of diamonds reversed, when seen, implies the lovers, organized by the air of Pentacles, inverted–a decision has been made, and the conception of its results will take the full cycle of the moon, or 30 days.

When we learn to read the Tarot this way, then we do not need to memorize all 56 minor cards individually. It becomes easier to identify the meanings behind each suit and each number, and then to pair them up together to create the true message being told. Remember that when reading the Tarot, we also interpret reversed cards as an alternative or inverted meaning, on account of the blind nature of love. Remember that spells work on the causal plane, and when guided by intuition, provide faith for emotional and mental changes to influence etheric and physical results. We may be presented a card to read in our dreams by the Deities of higher dimensions and should rely on our knowledge of the Tarot to take intuitive action on what is necessary for us, given our experiences and life circumstances.

I myself follow the Egyptian Tarot, where the Fool card is no longer a zero, and is regarded as the number 77–a Minor Arcanum, when reduced to five, signifies change. Therefore, the real count begins at one, and the 22nd Major Arcanum exists hidden from the general public. I reveal it to you here, the Major Arcanum 22/Return: Truth, Illumination, Perfection.

Every person reads their Tarot in their own way and the depth of study is immersive. It is a highly intuitive practice that requires patience and an open mind but not intellectualization. Taking your time to learn the core concepts is widely beneficial to helping you read with ease. It often doesn't take more than three minutes while a single reading can leave a lifelong impression. So, it isn't about rushing or trying to understand everything to the maximum. Tarot is about the divination of yourself. By achieving a divine formula of communication within yourself you will find confidence in achieving a fulfilling life.

Witchcraft Magick Spells

Chapter 6

Mantra, Incantation, Meditation

"When we use words, we are manipulating the vibrations of the objects, striking the essence of its existence and awakening the spirits within it."

Magick words are the most ineffable tools that a witch has. When her intentions are brought to life through the belief and practical faith of her own power she is striding confidently through the stars of the sky. By using magickal words to create a spell, we set forth intentions that we wish to bring to life, and that is the purest form of energy work and magick. Witches use several different means of constructing words to reverberate the consciousness into activity. Depending on the style of witchcraft, a witch may decide to charm something small like a bracelet, or she might speak some healing words as she's preparing her potion or tea. Any and all things that a witch decides to do will be brought to life when she speaks. What she charms will have purpose and meaning as she works towards creating real change in her life.

Incantations

When we perform an incantation, what we are truly doing is charming something with pure energy for a specific purpose. Using clairvoyance, as you speak the words of your spell, what you wish to manifest and bring to life will ultimately charm anything. There are many small and simple incantation spells used to charm the ears of wandering minds to inspire the imagination to enlightened feelings of purity and gratitude.

We can use our magickal powers to help someone overcome struggles, heal physically and mentally, or succeed in obtaining a better career, to name a few examples. Our magickal words have power, and when we imbue objects, such as books, sigils, gemstones, herb tinctures, or candles, for example, we are putting a purpose to those items so that they may help us harness powers of comprehension to take necessary action.

Tracy Addams

When we use words, we are manipulating the vibrations of the objects, striking the essence of its existence and awakening the spirits within it. By casting intentions with purpose, like a feather into a nest, or a drop of rain on the earth--a witches constant application of loving harmony creates warmth and comfort in the microscale, while also harnessing the immense power of nature at the macroscale.

Mantras

A mantra is a set of words that we say to ourselves to reinforce our positive beliefs and make room for growth. Mantras are affirming and strong, and as we speak them on a daily basis we open the doors of our future so that like Genies we become graced with the opportunity to grant wishes. Mantras need to come from our hearts and when spoken orally they act as a gong--awakening the consciousness. The elementals of the earth--those very small beings of consciousness who live in the plants, yes, the fairies and nymphs, respond to mantras and illuminate us when we invite them to help us. This deeper knowledge of who we are and what we want to become can bring forth the correct energies to not only make our words true but to allow them to flourish and take on a life of their own.

A mantra should always start out positively with focus on the good that can come. This amazing phenomenon of mantra is enhanced with the harmonious partnership between body and spirit. When we let ourselves realize the impact of sacred geometry in the body, our mantras are enhanced. Normally done while sitting down, here is a practice done standing up. The mantra "Fa" when spoken in combination with both arms raised forwards and the left a little higher than the right, brings the solar rays of dawn to enlighten the spirit within. The mantra, although it is quite a silly one, is completely intuitive, and shouldn't be analyzed with anything but the heart of a child.

Continue to recite, *Faaaa, Feeee, Fiiii, Foooo, Fuuuu,* three times. With the body in the shape of an F, this is also a sacred rune. The deity who helps with this mantra is Isis, who is sometimes pictured with her wings in this shape. And so when invoking her help, pray like this:

"Universal force, oh powerful deity, you who ignite my divine fire and irradiate it through the cosmos, let your sacred flame blaze within me so that I may pass my light to all who I come into contact with."

Meditation

Meditation calms us and centers us so that we can prepare ourselves for performing rituals and spells. A spell is only as powerful and possible as a witch allows it to be. Without having clear intentions and an uncluttered mind a witch will not be able to bring forth good and positive change in her life. She could be clinging to self-doubt, which will bleed into her practice and leave room for mistakes and failures. Meditation allows us to learn to love ourselves

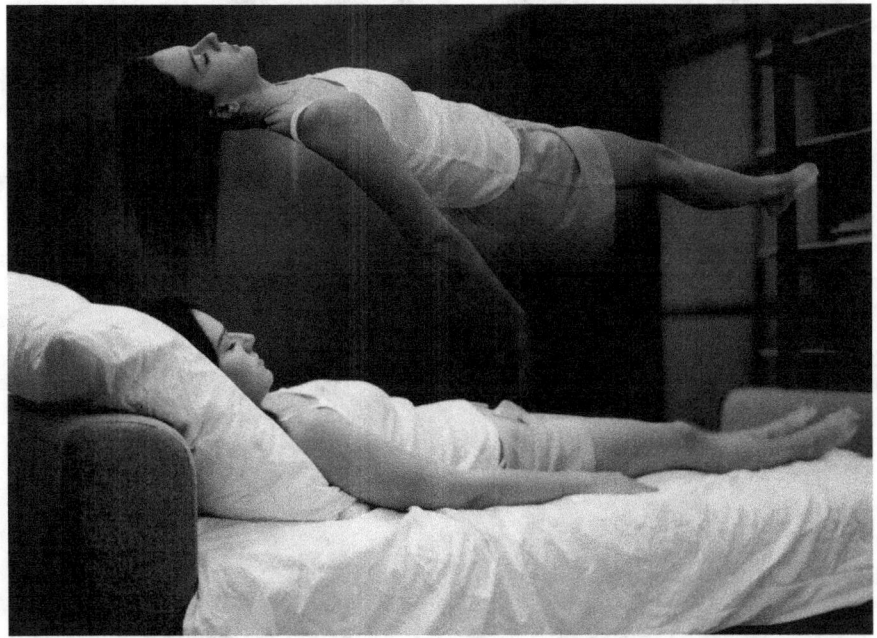

as we gain confidence in freeing ourselves from any negative thought patterns. The abuse of psychoactive substances should be refrained by the witch, as this only leads to dependency, and failure in her practices. A witch should seek enlightenment, harmony, and inner fulfillment, not the attainment of psychic powers for flaunting on the street.

A witch's mind, resplendent in calmness and tranquility after meditation, will not be burdened by interruption, emergency or jealous attack. Her faculties of wisdom in flexibility and comprehension will allow her to speak with clarity, act compassionately, and protect with absolute distinction.

Tracy Addams

Words Have Power

When conducting a spell or a ritual, a witch must have clarity and conviction in what she is working to produce. All words have immense power, even when we aren't bewitching an item or speaking mantras for our personal well-being. The sooner that a witch understands this and learns to use her words properly, the quicker her life can change for the better. It is up to her to say to the world what she wants, and when she trusts in her own power, she is able to accomplish anything. So mote it be.

Chapter 7:

Herbalism, Herbs, Elementals, Tonics, Potions, Tinctures, Oils, Aromatherapies

Herbs and plants assist a witch in harnessing her intention with practical means according to the properties of the plants she is using. The specific magickal properties of common herbs along with their physiological influences on the human body are listed within this chapter. Each herb has a specific characteristic flavor, akin to its psychological effect in a spell. It may be sweet, sour, salty, pungent or bitter. Using any or all of these herbs in our spell work is vital, and with gradual practice a witch's herbal experience will be complete with knowledge of many more. We can add these to our meals and consume them or incorporate them into our spells as minor sacrifices to the deities we intuitively find connection with.

Herbalism, Herbs, Elementals, Tonics, Potions, Tinctures, Oils, Aromatherapies

Herbs can be formed into tonics, tinctures, and balms, or as oils used for things like aromatherapies. When desired, tonics enable long-term repetitive use for certain spells. Tonics are very potent teas which we can drink–they are sometimes known as brews. Tonics are made with the leaves, flower petals or hips, roots, or stalk, and they are strained into boiling water. Their aim is to tone or cleanse the body to enhance the involvement and experience of a spell.

Tinctures are concentrated liquids that are made with grain alcohol or vinegar and plant parts.[i] The alcohol draws out the pure components of the plant to create a highly concentrated tincture without boiling anything. They are shelf-stable, lasting a long time. Chamomile is an excellent herb I create tinctures with, as it can be used to treat symptoms of anxiety and inflammation with a few drops under the tongue once a day.

Balms are creamy, slightly oily mixtures that are made with dried herbs, a carrier oil, and a hardening component like beeswax. Balms made with

Calendula help to heal cuts and scrapes, while Aloe Vera gel and Lemon balm make great burn ointments.

Aside from creating and experimenting with your own herbal mixtures, we might simply use a specific herb in our spell to work with the elemental inside its cellular structure. This is a spiritual practice and should include prayer, and offerings. In addition, witches hang herbs throughout their home and place them in jars to let them dry to harmonize with the essence within the plant. Using an herb in our food or tea should be considered for its ability to assist us spiritually, to cleanse our palate, and to set our mood.

Let's look at some of the popular herbs and plants that mother nature offers, as well as what they can do to help us create the lives we wish to live.

Bitter Herbs and Flowers

Bitterness is often described as a sharp flavor that is rarely sweet or salty. This taste is similar to the way unsweetened cocoa powder or black coffee leave a stark flavor in the mouth. Many herbs are found to be bitter, mostly because green plants are naturally unsweet.

Aloe

Aloe is a succulent plant that provides luck, peace, and protection.

Calendula

This herb flowers with blooms that smell of sweet spice and honey, but when dried, calendula becomes bitter. Protection, psychic abilities, and legal matters can all be helped with calendula.

Chamomile

Chamomile is a beautifully white and fragrant flower that is said to calm someone and allow them to rest.

Heather

Heather is a slightly bitter herb that offers luck, protection, immortality, and peace.

Mugwort

Mugwort is used in spells associated with divination and dreaming. It is also connected to digestive health.

Peppermint

Peppermint is an herb that cleanses and protects. It also aids in digestion.

Rose

Rose has a bright, floral flavor that enhances beauty, sexuality, and romance. This primarily bitter flower can sometimes be a little sweet depending upon the type of rose.

Sweet Herbs and Flowers

Some herbs and flowers carry a sweet flavor. They often have a hint of savoriness as well and are put into comfort foods on many occasions. As opposed to green vegetables, which are generally bitter, typical sweet eats are fats and sugars. With herbs and flowers, the spiritual elementals offer their divine influence in sweetness, which helps with digestion and hormone processing in the spleen. Young or old witches will usually enjoy sweet, festive flavors.

Anise

Anise is a sweet spice with the flavor of licorice. It's best for creating and boosting happiness, as well as purifying the unwanted energies from your space.

Bay Leaf

Bay leaf is a pine and minty mix of an herb. Known to help with prosperity and to break curses, this herb is great for wealth and protection.

Cinnamon

One of the most well-known spices, cinnamon is capable of protection, wealth, love, happiness, and psychic abilities.

Daisy

Daisies are edible flowers that have a sweet, sometimes nutty flavor. They are known to help with love and luck and are connected to babies.

Jasmine

Jasmine is a widely popular herb and flower that is used to enhance teas. It is known to help with love, attraction, and sexuality.

Lavender

Lavender is a highly popular and beneficial herb that can heal, offer protection, bring peace, provide sleep and resolve headaches, and enhance love. It is a woodsy, delicate scent that witches use in everything from teas to balms.

Lemon Balm

Lemon balm is great for healing and for bringing peace to your surroundings. Lemon balm is also known to amplify psychic abilities

Lily

Lilies are fragrant, sweet, and bright flowers that can provide renewal, happiness, fertility, and opulence.

Marjoram

Marjoram is a light and delicate herb that is related to mint and oregano. It provides cleansing properties and can remove negativity. It also helps with love and wealth.

Nutmeg

Nutmeg is a warm and nutty spice that offers protection and luck. It is also great at breaking hexes and amplifying intelligence.

Rosemary

Rosemary helps with health issues including circulation and cognition. It is also connected with sea magick. Rosemary has a subtle pine flavor that goes well with its lemony flavor.

Sour Herbs and Flowers

Sour herbs and flowers are flavorful and bright, often citrusy too. They are used in everything from fragrances to teas, and provide great cleansing benefits. Sour flavors often moisten the palate, and soften cross moods. Not to be over-used by empaths, sour herbs promote the movement of bodily fluids, and should be handled carefully as witches need to protect themselves too. Helpful for those in sour moods to open up.

Bergamot

Bergamot is a citrusy fruit that is thought to be a natural hybrid of oranges and lemons. It is a bright green and small fruit. Bergamot is used for better sleep, to enhance success and power, and to provide protection.

Vervain

With a slightly bitter and citrusy profile, vervain goes well in desserts and teas. Purification, protection, and warding off evil are associated with this herb. It is also believed to help reduce stress and amplify astral divination.

Pungent Herbs and Flowers

Pungent herbs and flowers have a strong scent and flavor that are unmistakably potent, sometimes resulting in a sneeze. They are often used in smaller amounts because they add a strong heat to the meal or mixture they are in. They produce a numbness in the tongue, and sometimes also perspiration, suggesting a certain hormonal effect on the pores of the skin. They relieve coughing but need to be handled carefully to avoid regurgitation from the oils inside them.

Chili Peppers

Chili peppers are a group of vegetables and plants that offer many diverse flavors and smells. Most are described as smokey, earthy, or spicy. Chili peppers aid in love and devotion, and they are known to break hexes.

Eucalyptus

Eucalyptus is a plant that offers protection, inspiration, health, and purification. It has a sharp, yet mellow scent of pine and citrus.

Ginger

Ginger has a bold, sweet, but also warm flavor that is put into everything from stir fry meals to teas. Ginger boosts confidence, prosperity, adventures, and new beginnings.

Juniper

Juniper is a piney, peppery flavored and scented plant. Its berries are used in a variety of drinks and decorations. Juniper is associated with health and love. It is also able to banish and protect.

Oregano

Strength, joyfulness, liveliness are all embodied in the plant oregano. With a combination of bitter and spice, oregano has an earthy flavor that can come off strong in some meals.

Patchouli

As an herb of abundance, patchouli is known to aid in wealth, love, and fertility. It also helps to keep one grounded. This herb is often described as spicy or earthy, and it has a warm, bold aroma.

Sage

Sage is a well-known herb that can banish and repel negativity when consumed. It also offers wisdom, peace, wishes, and immortality as a tea. It may also improve memory and cognition.

Thyme

Thyme is an earthy herb that has a hint of lemon and mint. It helps with relationships and reputation, and can also boost wealth.

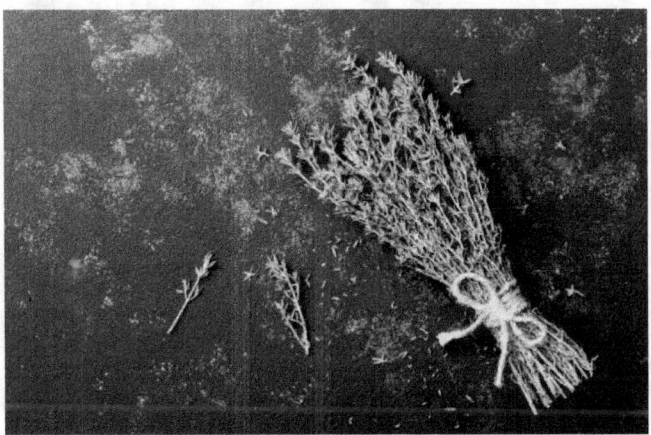

Salty Herbs and Flowers

Salty tasting herbs and flowers are made to help with dissolving hard conceived ideas, drying out moisture, and removing phlegm. Their effect is actually to balance the kidneys and help the body metabolize sodium. They taste delicious and leave a natural thirst in the mouth.

Basil

Basil is a bright green plant that offers protection and wealth. It is also able to invoke love. Basil is put on many foods, and it is used as a replacement for salt.

Dill Weed

Dill weed is an herb that aids in protection, wealth, and attraction. It's a full-flavored herb that is often used with pickles and dressings.

Parsley

Parsley is known to help with strength, and it can increase one's luck and wealth.

Tracy Addams

Herbs Are Magickal

What's necessary in the study of ourselves is to study our human nature. Without becoming slaves to our five senses, we can study our moods and use herbs and flowers to deliver a desired effect. Anything that we see, hear and touch are appraised of by common interactions throughout our daily lives. But even more intimate are the subtleties of our real lives experience with taste and smell. The sound of crackling fire may alert us to either a feeling of safety or danger depending on the current environment in which we stand; however, the smell of victory or taste of defeat are unmistakable internal states of consciousness. As we re-orient our desires through spell casting efforts and divine intentions, herbs and flowers will begin to enlighten our lives, enhance feelings of passion, and heal tremendous wounds.

Witchcraft Magick Spells

Chapter 8

Earth Magick: Crystals, Gems, and Stones

"These can be used in spell jars, made into jewelry, placed on your altar, or carried with you in your secret pocket."

Witches use various types of stones and gems to achieve dominion over the earth element in their spells. Some gems are great for love and fertility, while others are more inclined to aid in communication and self-expression. There are many gemstones available across the planet, with some being more rare than others. Sometimes when a spell calls for a gem that you cannot seem to find, it is okay to replace it with something similar based on its qualifying vibrations.

As a general rule of thumb, gemstones have properties that are associated with their color or the element they are linked with. For example, the color orange corresponds to creativity and curiosity. Orange gemstones are abundant in joyfulness and warmth, and they bring us energies that boost our passions and uniqueness. Likewise, stones linked to the elements, such as the water-linked moonstone, have similar properties to that element. Moonstone is an emotional and feminine stone that protects and cleanses just like water.

Let's take a look at some of the most well-known and widely used gemstones in witchcraft. These can be used in spell jars, made into jewelry, placed on your altar, or carried with you in your secret pocket.

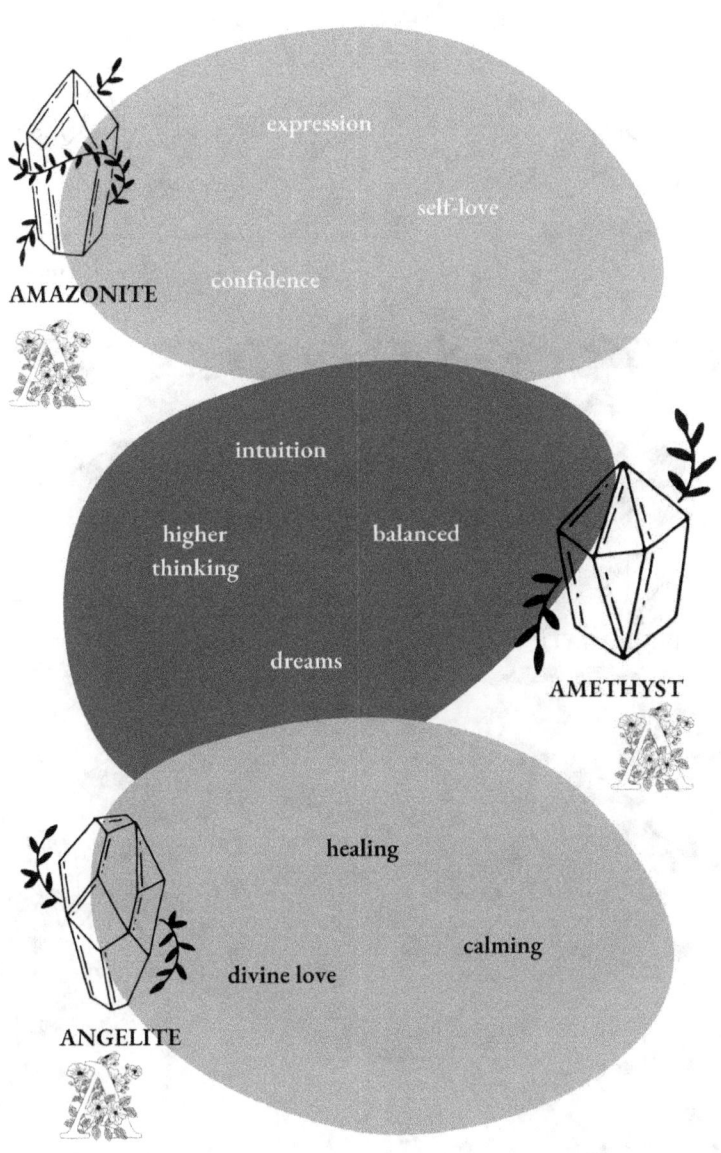

Witchcraft Magick Spells

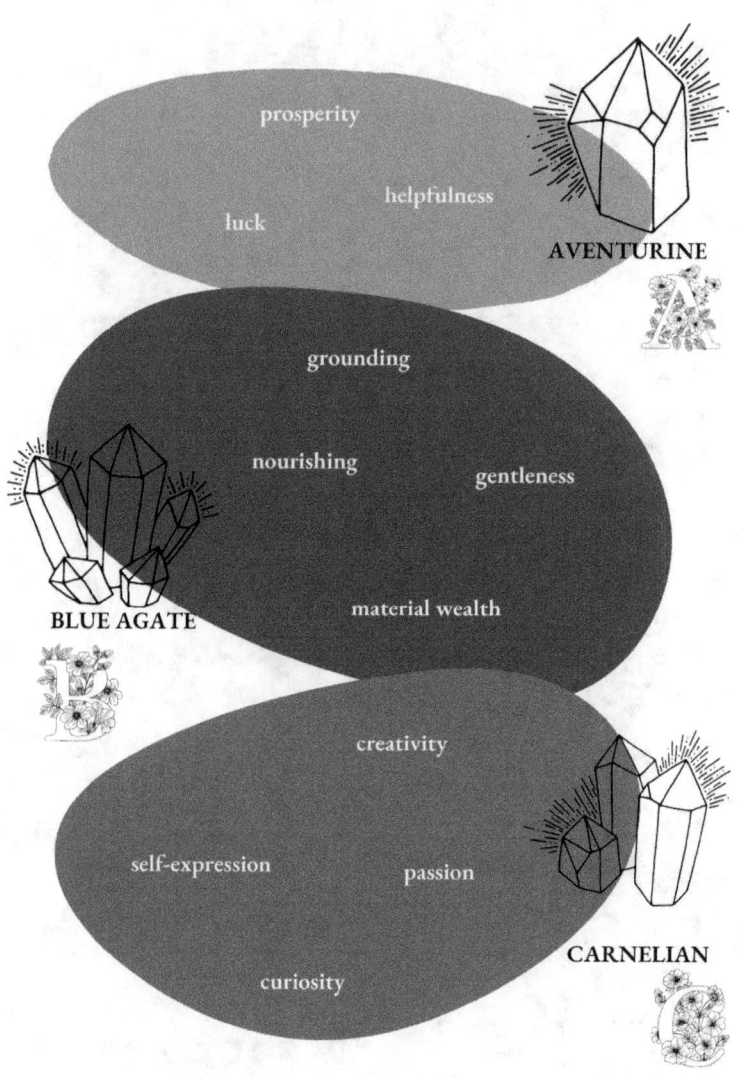

Tracy Addams

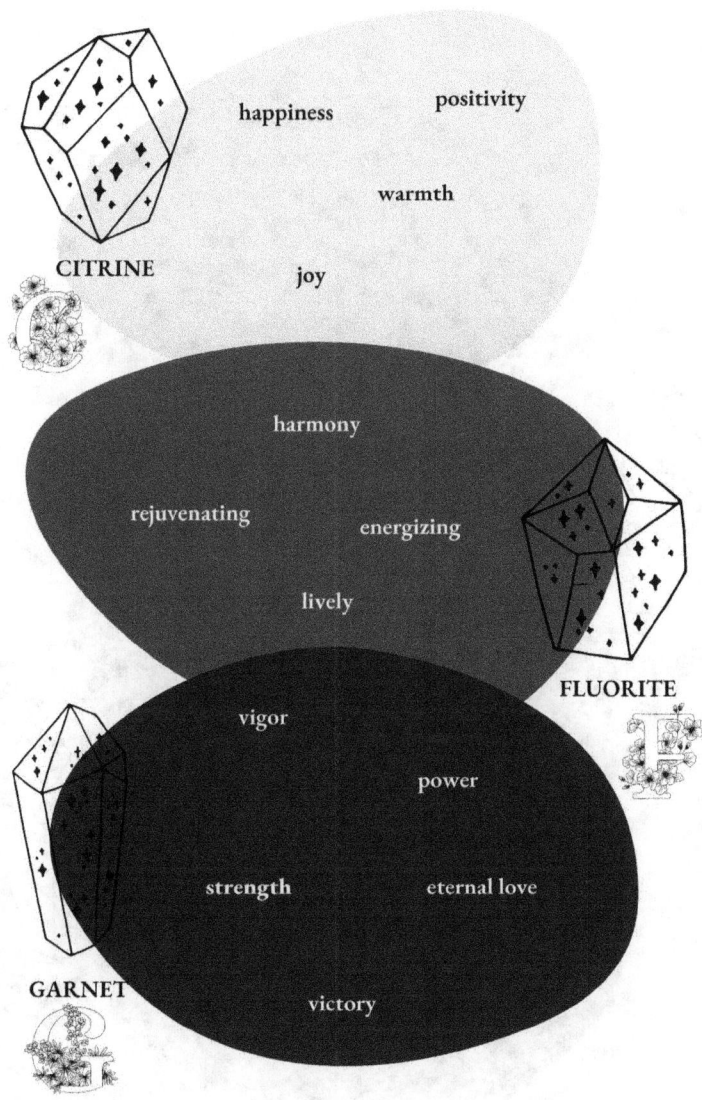

Witchcraft Magick Spells

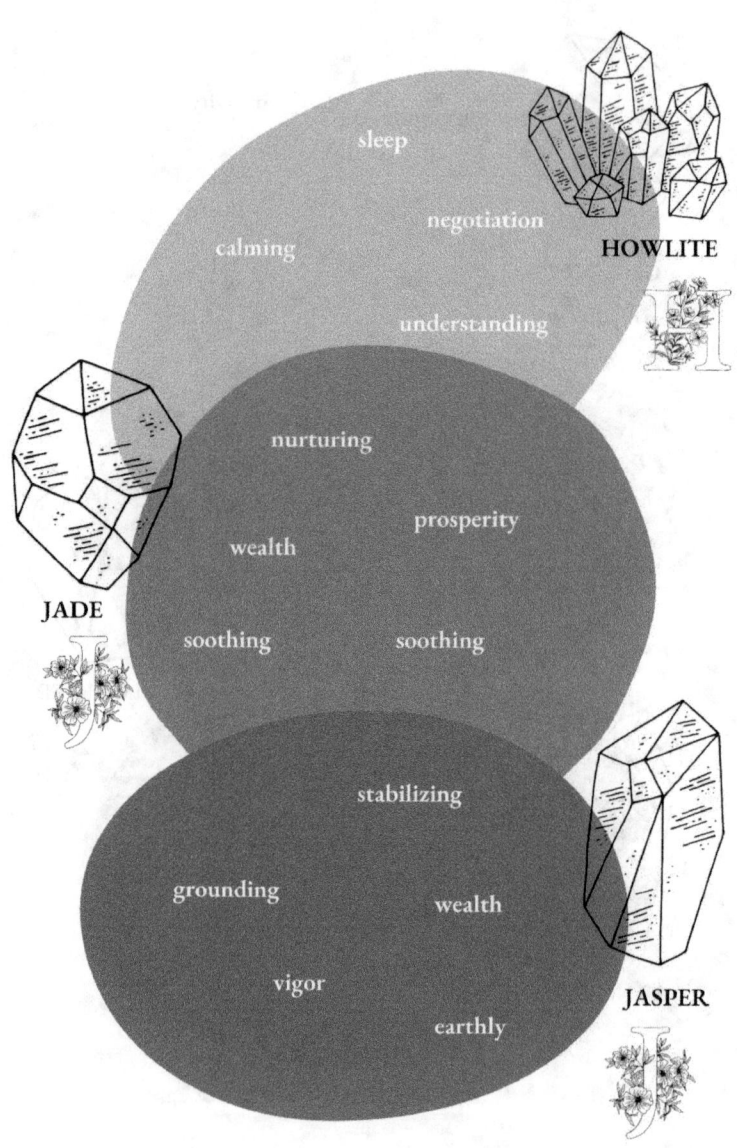

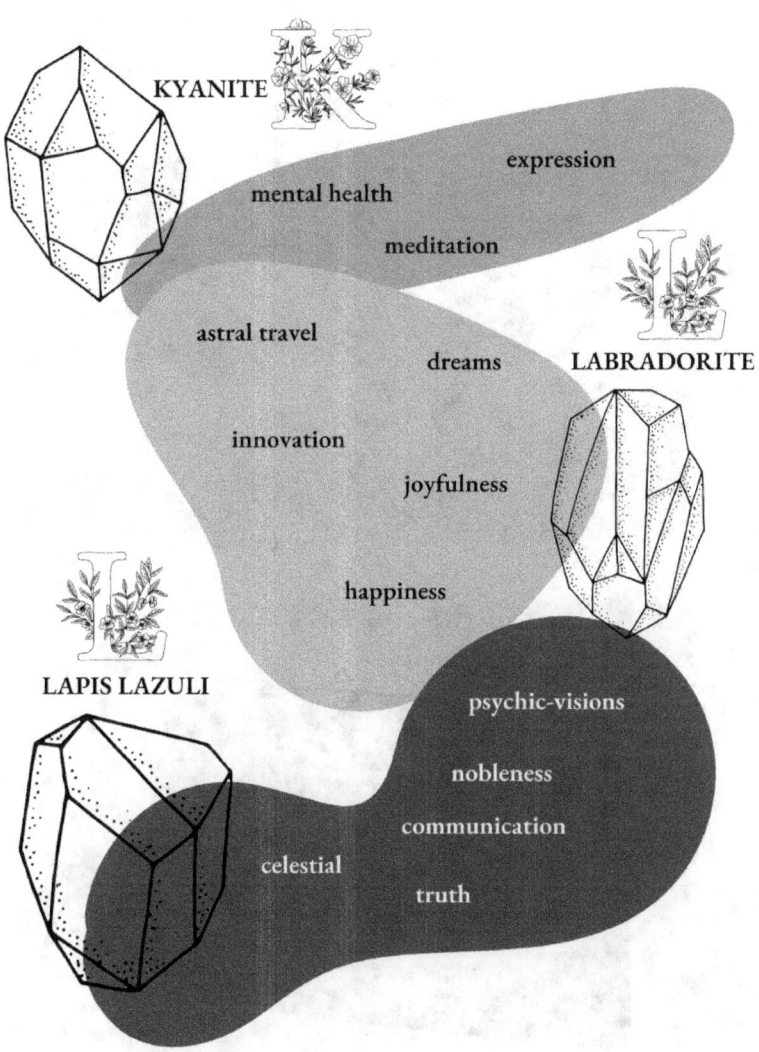

Witchcraft Magick Spells

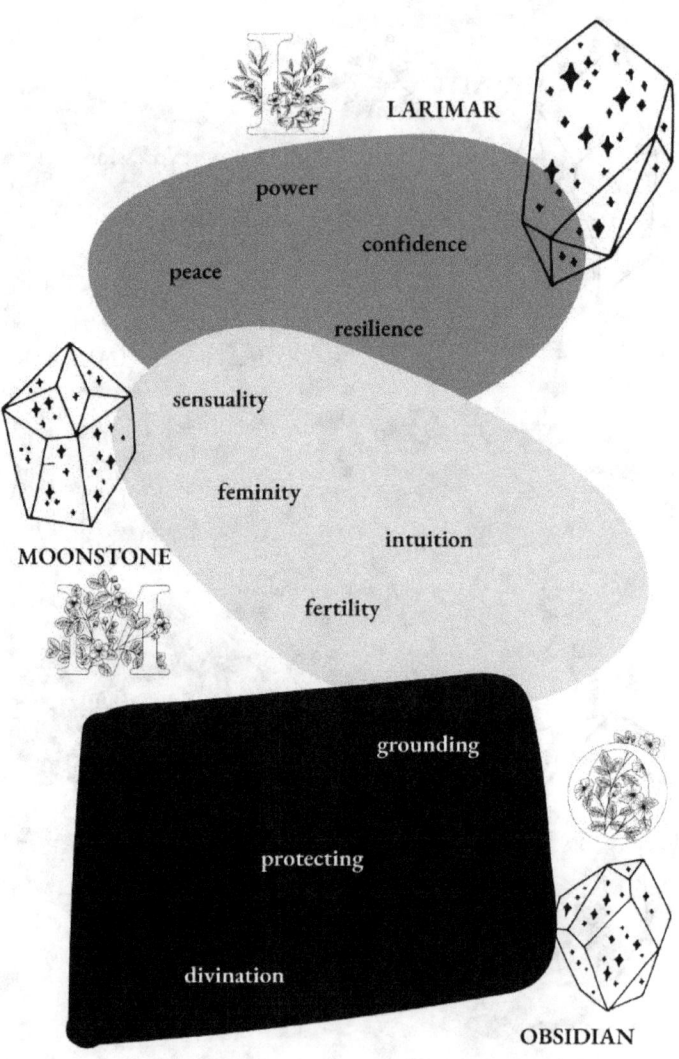

LARIMAR
- power
- confidence
- peace
- resilience

MOONSTONE
- sensuality
- feminity
- intuition
- fertility

OBSIDIAN
- grounding
- protecting
- divination

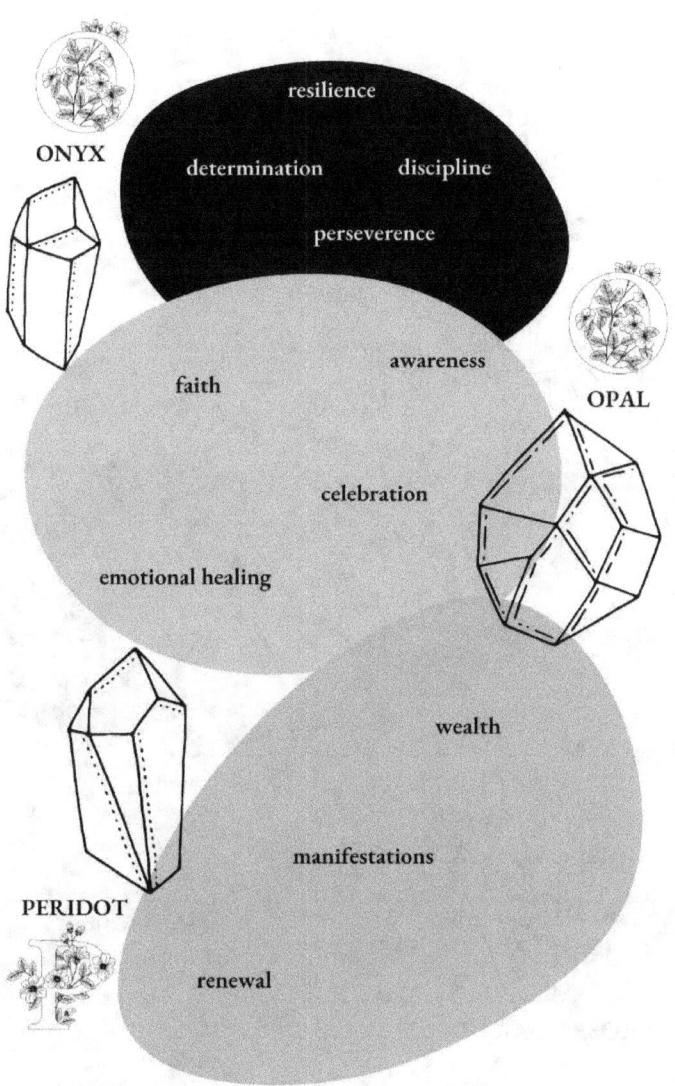

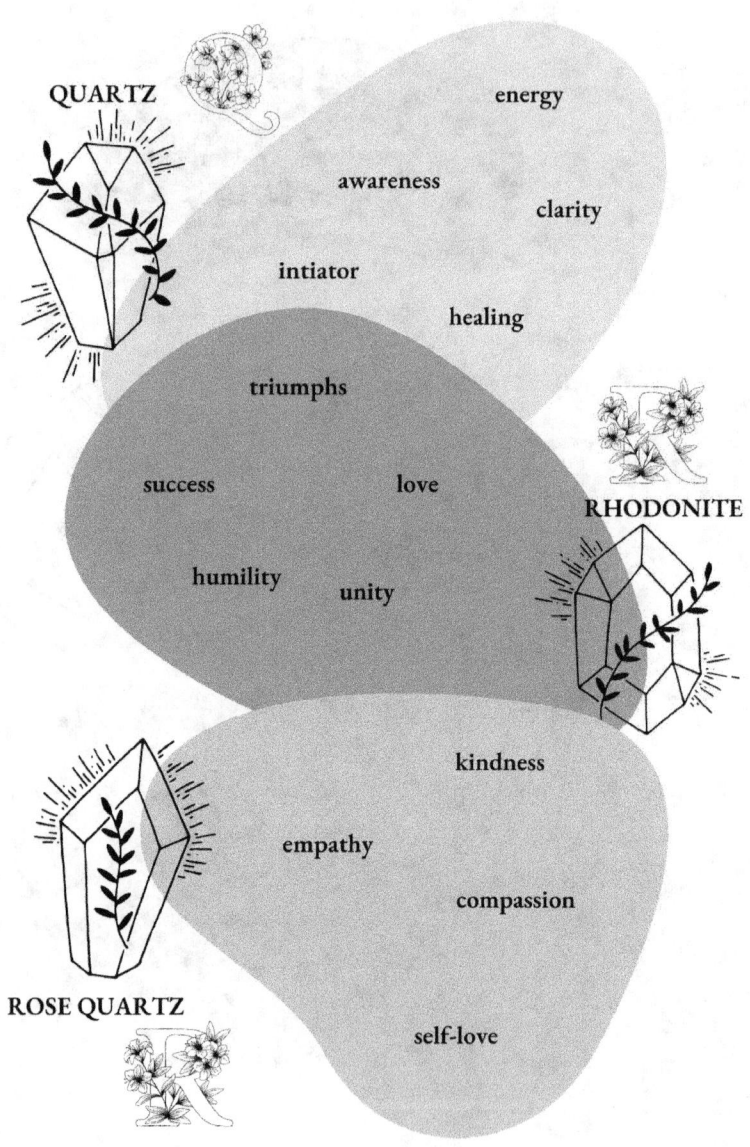

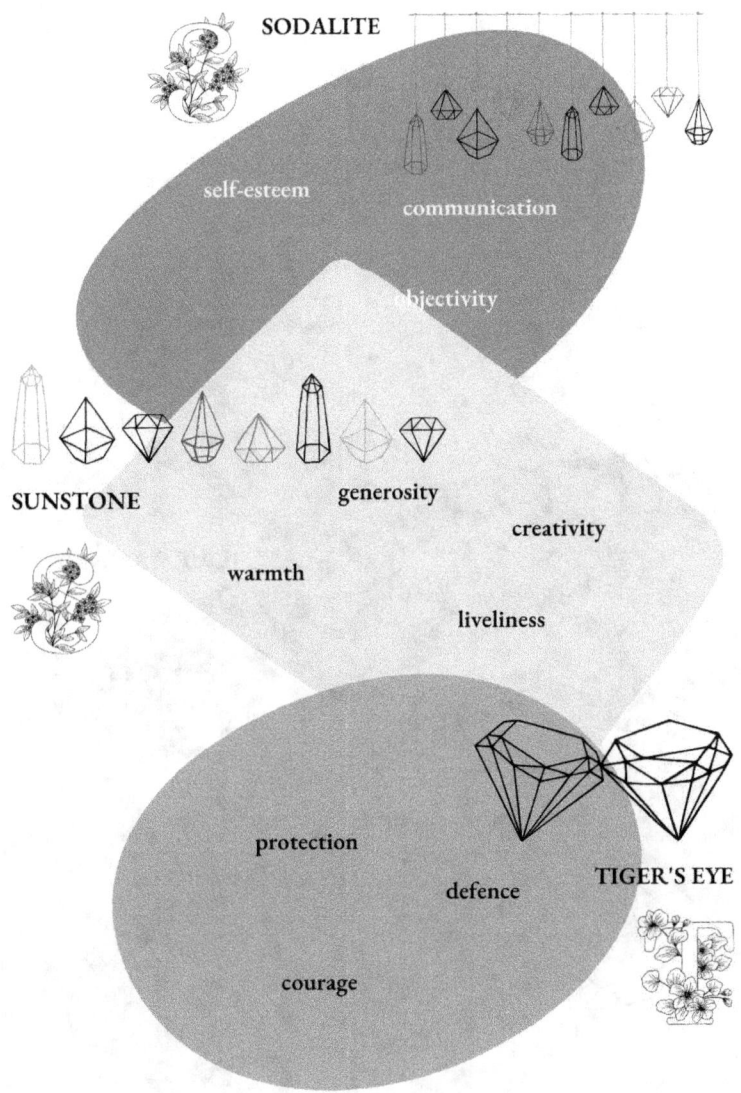

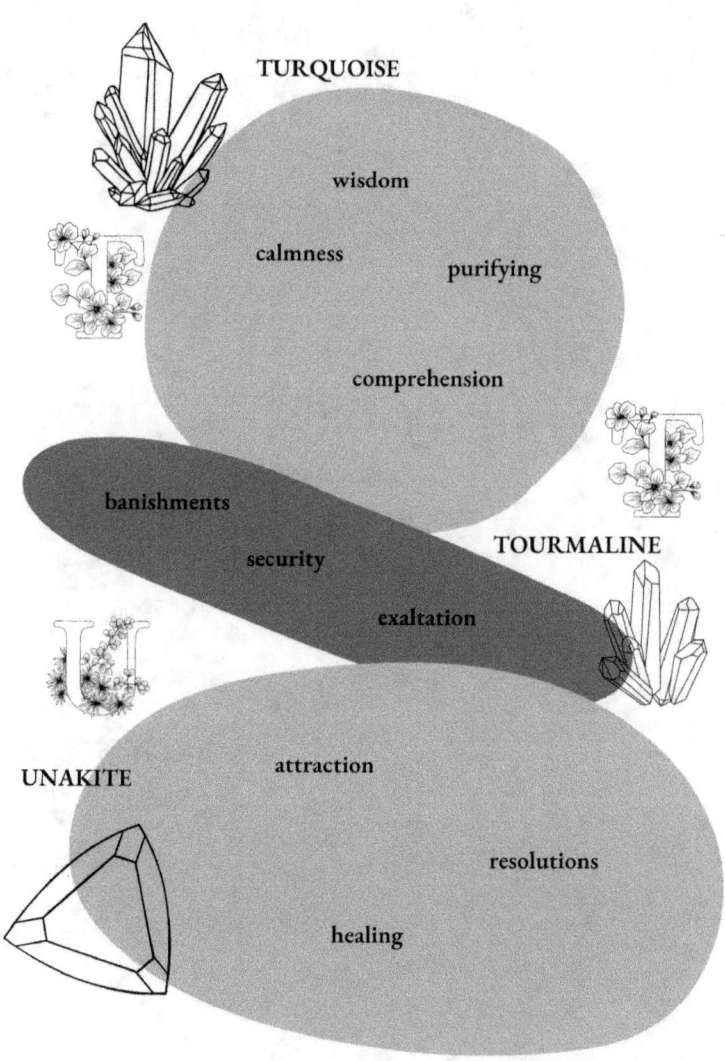

We have gone through the basic knowledge of our witchcraft magick spell ingredients and learned how nature offers an abundance of opportunity we can partner with as we learn about manifesting our dreams through our intentions. We are now ready to create and cast some life-changing spells.

PART III

SPELLS

In this part of the book, we'll be looking at all the different spells that can make a positive impact in our lives. Practicing these spells will allow us to connect with our desired spiritual Deities, thereby channeling their wisdom towards our purpose. Having clearly defined intentions is everything, and so every witch should learn to be precise in her projections of fire with her words, her empathetic ear to hear the call of the Divine, her creative signals manipulating the sexual waters, and her heartbeat vibrations quaking from the Earth. This is how a witch embodies her presence at the altar–with Deities and Mother Nature as her colleagues.

Preparing Your Spells

To perform a spell, we must first create a space with balance between feminine and masculine energies–one of harmony. We do this by casting a circle. The purpose of our circle is to engage the consciousness of our loving decisions, to ward off attack from black magicians, and to engender feelings of confidence in our intentions.

We begin by cleansing our space. Depending on the type of spell you are casting, you may simply use your altar, or you may want to spread out and use a larger space like a well-ventilated room. Maybe you'll even perform your spell outside under the canopy of stars. In cleansing, I recommend a bell or chime, along with burning incense, like sulfur – a yellow powder that when burned heals the afflicted from addictions. Other items you may find worth choosing from are:

- Crystals like selenite to tap
- Sage bundles to burn
- Spraying of moon water
- Sprinkling of black salt
- Scribing sigils in the dirt

- Dusting with feathers

Advanced witches may want to spray fiery alcohol or use torches to cleanse the air and ward off unwanted touches. Using your wand, athame, or simply your hands, draw out your circle in your space. Again, your circle can be as large or small as you need it to be, but be sure to make room for yourself and others when present.

Envision the circle coming to life, creating a protective barrier of light and strength around you. Motion to build your circle in a clockwise manner as you say the following words in the directions in which you are facing.

I call upon the spirits of the north and the Genies of earth. I call upon the spirits to the east and the Genies of air. I call upon the spirits to the south and the Genies of fire. I call upon the spirits to the west and the Genies of water.

As you complete your circle, say, *I call upon the spirit of the Triple Moon Goddess. Now complete, I consecrate this circle.*

After this, you are now in a protective sphere that will allow you to easily perform your magick.

During the Spell

It is important to note a few things that occur during the spell itself. These things are up to you as you must use your own intuition, and they can change depending on your desires for the spell.

Candles: Simply light them with a match or another candle. When returning to light it again, either blow it out, snuff it, pick the wick with your fingers, or dip it in water. Each method has its own purpose. Blow out a candle and respect the wind in your spells, carry a feather to remind you. To snuff is to hide as a secret–be mindful of your memory spells going off-kilter. Pick a wick and develop your instinct to hunt, just remember to seek permission. Dipping candles is mixing fire with water, so respect your creative energies.

Gods/Goddesses: I suggest Deities to work with, both Gods and Goddesses, Priests and Priestesses, Masters and Mistresses, etc. This is not an exhaustive list, but be careful working with Deities you do not know. Get to know them, their story, and what they will help you with before summoning them to your altar or elsewhere.

After the Spell

Sometimes we make offerings to the Gods and Goddesses during our spells. This isn't always necessary, but it does help to win their favor and enhance the outcomes. The Gods and Goddesses will express thanks in ways you will realize for years to come. For example, Anubis is summoned in times of surgery or when moving from one home to another, as a traveler. Represented as the jackal, I offer to him Hematite and Myrrh while invoking his assistance. After the spell, I dispose of the ashes and cleanse my hematite with a selenite wand.

Cleansing Your Space

Once your spell is complete, it is important to close your circle and release the spirits you called upon. When we close the circle after the spell is finished, we do the same steps as opening the circle but in reverse.

Begin by motioning to unwind your circle in a counterclockwise fashion. As you face each direction, speak the following words.

I thank the Triple Moon Goddess and release her spirit from this circle. I release the spirits to the west and the Genies of water. I release the spirits to the south and the Genies of fire. I release the spirits to the east and the Genies of air.

I release the spirits of the north and the Genies of the Earth. I thank you all and end this circle.

After you finish, you can clean up your things and put away your tools and unused items.

Tracy Addams

Witchcraft Magick Spells

Chapter 9

Love and Romance

Spells that help us find love and romance are designed to attract the right mate for us. When our mate is found, he or she will ignite the marvelous force of love within us. When we are capable of loving ourselves in every way possible, this will be a great mix. When a mate is desired, we need to clearly define what attributes we want to attract. Casting a love spell is performed by acknowledging our intentions and delivering them the Divine for assistance. With the correct ingredients and invocations, marvelous outcomes result.

True Love Jar Spell

This true love jar spell allows the witch to attract affection in ways she desires. It will bring forth the right energies to allow us to meet the person that is right for us. It might open the door for someone we already know or someone we have feelings for but aren't sure how they feel yet. It might also create space in our life to allow a new person to come through and sweep us off our feet!

Optimal Timing:

A love spell like this will work best if it is started during the waxing moon. At this time, we are preparing for growth and new possibilities. We are looking to increase our fortunes and favors, and to bring forth a wonderful time of abundance as the full moon nears. Since we might be working on this spell over several days, compiling it piece by piece at the start of the waxing moon will enable us to complete it during the full moon.

Gods/Goddesses:

Romance Deities can help to enhance your spell and make it a reality. We can ask Freya, the Norse Goddess of love and war, to help guide us as we construct this jar spell. Freya is connected to beauty and fertility, and she watches over the sea. Her control over the waters of sex will lift the weight of this spell to float and set us sailing with the strength, emotion, and love we desire.

Ingredients:

Pink candle

Moonstone

Tracy Addams

Rose quartz chips

Dried basil

Jasmine essential oil

Small glass jar with a cork

String, leather, or hemp cord

Decorative pentacle

Primrose stems and flowers

Instructions:

Lay out all your items and take a deep breath to clear your mind.

Set out the primrose stems and flowers around the surface where you will construct the jar spell. Speak to Freya for her blessings. *Freya, bring me love and romance into my life.*

Light the candle and pray: *Oh warming fire of romance, may it burn bright and ignite passion.*

Begin assembling your jar spell. Add the moonstone to the jar as you say, *blanket me with love.*

Sprinkle the basil into the jar and over the moonstone. *Provide harmony to me.*

Add the rose quartz chips. *Let my inner beauty shine.*

Drop in a few drops of the jasmine essential oil. *I desire intimacy and love.*

Close the jar with a cork. *I bring everything together as one.*

Tie your charm around the neck of the jar. Melt your pink candle wax over the cork to create a permanent seal. Continue with your intentions. *I seal this spell and welcome my true love.*

Close your spell by thanking Freya for her wisdom. *Freya, thank you for sealing this spell with your love.*

Extinguish the candle during this time, then cleanse your space.

Keep the jar somewhere that it won't break, such as on a bookshelf, a windowsill, or on a mantle. If others can see it, then we are ready for it to come true.

Self-Love Candle Spell

Sometimes we need a little bit of self-love in order to move forward in our lives. As we all have heard before, we cannot expect someone to love us if we cannot love ourselves. This simple spell doesn't necessarily need a sacred circle, and it can be done in a quick few minutes for instant relief.

Optimal Timing:

The new moon is the best time for a self-love spell. A new moon helps to inspire innocence. At this stage in the cycle, the mind is calm and curious, ready for new feelings to evolve and self-nurturing is ideal.

Gods/Goddesses:

Perhaps the most well-known Deity of love is Aphrodite. This Greek Goddess is the overseer of love and beauty, and most importantly, she is known as a Goddess of self-love. She enjoys offerings of sweet honey and soft roses. Providing an offering to Aphrodite will ensure you gain her favor as you cast your spell.

Ingredients:

Purple candle

Paper

Pencil

A flat, metallic plate with lipped edges works best

Rose petals in red or pink

Instructions:

Sprinkle the rose petals around the area you are working in and speak to Aphrodite. *Aphrodite, I ask you to join me in this spell as I open my heart to myself.*

Write these words on the paper: *I am worth it, I am mighty, I have divinity in my heart.*

Light your candle, and pray like this:. *With this flame, my eyes see love.*

Fold your paper and pass it through the flame to light the corner. Continue with your intentions. *Now my eyes are free to love myself again.*

Set the paper into the dish and allow it to burn out to ashes. Extinguish the candle.

At this time, thank Aphrodite for her presence and part ways. *Aphrodite, your love is my love eternally.*

You can now clean your items for another time.

Love Bracelet Spell

Sometimes we need to carry our love with us. This simple bracelet spell is one you can throw together in as little as an hour, and then it'll be with you to attract love and romance for years. Perfect for those already in a relationship, this bracelet can help keep your love passionate and abundant.

Optimal Timing:

Love spells like this one are best performed during the growing phases of the moon's cycle. The waxing moon, which is just after the new moon, up until the full moon. This makes way for growth and new possibilities. In addition, love spells do well in the spring when nature is fertile and seeds are planted.

Gods/Goddesses:

Hathor is the perfect Goddess to ask for assistance. She is an Egyptian Goddess of love, beauty, and pleasure. She helps to bring prosperous and satisfying love into anyone's life. Hathor's offerings are figs, dates, cedar, and turquoise.

Ingredients:

String, leather or hemp cord

Two round rose quartz beads

Dates or a turquoise stone

Instructions:

Set out the dates and turquoise as you ask Hathor to sit with you during the spell. *Hathor, sit with me and bless this bracelet for romance and passion.*

Wrap your cording material around your wrist six times. This will provide enough length for braiding.

Fold the cording material until you have four equally divided strings. At one end, tie a simple knot. At the other end, cut any strings that are looped so that you can braid the bracelet. You can braid with any type of knot that you admire. If you prefer to use a simple braid, make the bracelet with three divided strings rather than four.

Begin knotting and braiding the material as you repeat this mantra: *Come to me, the lover I seek. Two souls tied together, endlessly.*

Add a rose quartz bead one-third of the way through, then again at two-thirds of the way. These two beads symbolize unity, and the gems themselves increase romance and passion.

Tie off the bracelet with a clasp or a bead so that you can easily remove it. Alternatively, you can have someone help you tie it on your wrist so that it stays on tightly.

Thank Hathor for her support once you're finished. *Hathor, I am so grateful for your blessings.*

Meditative Soul Mate Spell

If you're searching for your soul mate, then this spell will help bring you both closer together. This person is not just someone who you can love, they are the perfect match for you in returning the love you seek to give. Finding this person will help you balance out your life, and in return, you will bring overwhelming joy and support to them. This spell is wonderful because you can customize it based on your tastes.

Optimal Timing:

Conducting this meditation spell during the new moon phase will help to open those doors that will lead you directly to your soul mate. During the new moon, we are looking forward to new growth and potential after the darkness of the last closing cycle. Meditating repeatedly during this time can also amplify your prospects as the stone will grow stronger with each session.

Gods/Goddesses:

We will ask Hathor to join us. She is a major Egyptian Goddess of love, song, dance, and sexuality with cow horns and a sun disk upon her head. She can enhance this meditation spell to help it flourish and brighten into a successful and bountiful spell. To connect best with Hathor, remember she likes mirrors and cosmetics, so use a staff, cane, or wand.

Ingredients:

One staff, cane, or wand made of smooth material free of dirt or frayed edges. It can be made of wood, bone, or stone.

Ylang ylang essential oil as its aroma inspires romance and a powerful, everlasting love.

Instructions:

Find a quiet space where you feel loved and comfortable. Sit and relax as you place the wand on a table or altar. Place a couple of drops of the essential oil onto it and allow it to dry. Clear your mind and take steady breaths as you let the fragrance fill your space.

Ask Hathor to join you in this meditation. *Hathor, I invite you to help bring me love and romance.*

After a couple of minutes, the wand will be dry, and you can hold it in your hand. Close your eyes and envision the life you want with your soul mate. Let the vision take hold before speaking the following words. *Two halves of a whole, two hearts divided. I welcome you, so our hearts may be united.*

After you are satisfied with your vision, you can open your eyes and thank Hathor. *Hathor, remember my vision, and mote it be.*

Keep your wand at your altar until you feel a new spark from someone. It might be a person you've never met, but it might also be an old flame or friend you haven't considered! Let your vision come to be, and continue to enhance the spell month to month with Hathor's help.

Love Potion Linen Spray

Once you've found someone that makes you happy, you might want to turn up the heat! This spell is one you can use anytime you're feeling like some extra romance. It has a wonderful fragrance that will entice your lover all night.

Optimal Timing:

Oshun, our romance Deity, is connected to Fridays, as she has historically received offerings on that day of the week. Putting together this spell on a Friday while you offer and connect with Oshun will bring you the most benefits. In addition, constructing this linen spray during a full moon will boost its love enchantments and provide a powerful concoction.

Gods/Goddesses:

Oshun is the African Ypruba Goddess of love and intimacy. She represents passion and devotion, also being a symbol of marriage. Oshun is known to enjoy honey, oranges, lemons, and pumpkins. She also likes mirrors.

Ingredients:

Small glass spray bottle (around 2 ounces)

Orange essential oil

Rose essential oil

Sandalwood essential oil

Ylang ylang essential oil

Alcohol-free Witch hazel

Distilled water

Red candle

Five fresh lemon slices

Instructions:

Set out the lemon slices as an offering for Oshun. She is associated with the number five, so five or more slices are important. Ask her to join you at this time. *Oshun, bless this love potion linen spray.*

Light the candle and then take a moment to visualize your love potion working as you implore its fragrances to inspire passion in the room.

Add a tablespoon of witch hazel to the bottle. Then add five or more drops of each essential oil. Finally, finish off the bottle with distilled water.

Tracy Addams

As you put the top on the bottle, say your intentions. *Love and romance, passion and desire. Fuel this love with intimate fire.*

At this time, thank Oshun and bid her farewell for your privacy. *Oshun, I am forever thankful for your magick touch.*

Blow out the candle and clean up your items. Keep the spray bottle in a cool, shaded spot in your room. Mist your sheets with a few spritzes whenever you want to heat up your love life! Also, this spray honestly works great in your car or out at a picnic, but be weary of camping as some scents attract wild animals.

Witchcraft Magick Spells

Chapter 10

Good Health and Prosperity

Living a prosperous life is not just about being comfortable, it is also about having the tenacity to get out to find the things that bring you health so that you can feel prosperous and full of satisfaction. Prosperity brings abundance and allows us to share our happiness with others and rejoice in community success. This is when we feel our spirits abound with gratefulness and accountability.

Healing Jar Spell

Create a healing jar spell for your home–this one uses lavender as the primary ingredient. Lavender grows in a dry arid climate, and has a namesake meaning "to wash." It's best to pick lavender in mid-spring when the stems are half covered in blooms. We are using lavender *essential oil* here, which you can buy, or make on your own.

Coupled with a few leaves of dried white sage, we have the namesake "heal" in our combination. This spell allows us to remain committed to our investment in ourselves, washing away the dust of hard work while letting healing take place. Amethyst acts as a crib, guarding the jar in its womb.

Optimal Timing:

Working this jar spell during the full moon will provide the highest rewards. The full moon allows for the most strength and power, enabling health in even difficult situations. In honor of Lugh, the God of harvest and health, create this jar spell around the autumn equinox. As the colder months set in, this spell will radiate your intention like a lamp in the darkness.

Gods/Goddesses:

Lugh is a Celtic Deity and is known as a healer God, though he is also associated with crafts and decorations. This makes him ideal for constructing an ornamental jar spell. Lugh accepts offerings of the harvest such as corn, herbs, and berries.

Ingredients:

White candle

Tracy Addams

Clear quartz crystal chips

Amethyst Geode

Dried white sage

Lavender essential oil

Small glass jar with a cork

Leather, hemp, or string

Pentacle Charm

Loose, dried corn

Instructions:

Lay out all your items and ask Lugh for his creative assistance. *Lugh, divine my will in my healing efforts.*

Light the candle and pray: *With this candle, I wash my spirit and I am healed.*

Begin assembling your jar spell. Add the clear quartz crystal chips to the jar and again pray: *My heart is healed.*

Sprinkle the sage into the jar and over the chips: *My mind is healed.*

Add four drops of lavender essential oil, then pray: *I am infused with health.*

Close the jar with a cork to pray: *I bring everything together as one.*

Tie your pentacle charm around the neck of the jar. Melt your white candle wax over the cork to create a permanent seal. Continue with your intentions. *I seal this spell, alive and well, to greet me here, year over year, a spell of health, now let's cheer.*

Place the jar into the amethyst geode.

Close your spell by thanking Lugh for his guidance. *Lugh, thank you for keeping my intentions clear.* Extinguish the candle during this time, then cleanse your space.

Healing Candle Spell

This candle spell takes very little set up, and the candle can be used over again to continue the healing intention. As always, a quiet and comfortable space is perfect, but this time I recommend you first cast a circle to free your mind of distraction because this healing spell requires focus.

Optimal Timing:

It is ideal to perform a candle spell for healing during the waxing moon, or even better, during a full moon, but it isn't necessary. The idea of new growth, which is associated with springtime, the morning, and the waxing moon, helps to create healthy pathways in your life. Either of these cycle times will amplify the spell you are working on to increase its potency.

Gods/Goddesses:

Summon Hygeia, the Greek Goddess of health, to direct your energy through this spell. She enjoys medicine, hygiene, and cleanliness, and likes the color blue. Hygeia can be offered vines or fresh fruit like blueberries. Because her symbol is the snake, giving her vines to climb is her favorite way to join you.

Ingredients:

Blue candle

Candle holder

Carving tool (toothpicks, pencils, clay tools, athame)

Vines

Fresh fruit

Instructions:

Clear your mind and sit comfortably in a chair within your sacred circle. Again, this is the type of spell that may benefit more after casting a sacred circle.

Sprinkle out the vines as you welcome Hygeia to come join you. *Hygeia, please come and sit with me as I focus my efforts on a healthy and happy future for (person's name).*

Using the carving tool, write the name of the person who needs healing into the candle.

Place the candle into a holder so that it is secure, then light the candle.

Speak your intentions or pray : *Flame so bright, heal (person's name) with light. Illness fades, health is made. In heart and mind; our souls, alive. Body strong, pain and worry, be gone.*

Allow the candle to burn for a moment as you close your eyes and envision the person as healthy and happy as they should be.

Thank Hygeia for her help. *Hygeia, remember us as we heal.*

Extinguish the candle and cleanse your things.

Keep the candle safe on a shelf in your bathroom to aid in good hygiene, set it in a sunny window to capture positive and healing light, or place it on a table as a centerpiece for when you are facing ailments. You can light it again to increase the power of the spell, speaking the same incantation as here. When you feel that the person is healthy and happy and that the candle is no longer needed, allow it to burn all the way out.

Tracy Addams

Good Health Necklace Spell

Necklaces are fun to make and can be customized in many different ways. Creating a necklace that can help you overcome health problems, whether they are mental or physical, is a fun craft that can also provide meditative peace. This necklace can also be made for other people as a gift.

Optimal Timing:

Creating this necklace during the full moon helps to release melatonin and promote healthy sleep cycles. We use kyanite crystal as its pendant for its ability to clear infections, relax muscles, and relieve pain. Anyone who wishes to improve their relationship with others should enjoy the harmony of making this necklace.

Gods/Goddesses:

Artemis is famous for helping women through childbirth, but she is also known as a healing Deity who can eliminate disease. She is intimately connected with the hunt, where Orion wooed her. We can offer Artemis items from her beloved forests like nuts, pine bark, honey, or feathers.

Ingredients:

Sterling silver chain with clasp

Kyanite with a loop or hole to fish the chain through

Walnuts

Instructions:

Remain light-hearted and happy as you invoke Artemis under the moonlight. *Artemis, I honor your precision and ask you to help me heal.* Set out the walnuts.

Thread the silver chain through the kyanite and say your intentions. *With my kyanite, I call for health.*

Thank Artemis for her amazing duty. *Artemis, your eyes are my eyes.* Now you can then use this necklace for as long as you wish.

Meditative Prosperity Spell

Prosperity is not just about luck and finance, it is also about having good health and longevity. With this meditative prosperity spell, we focus our efforts on boosting our health so that we can be confident and live long and happy lives. This spell is great for the young family, reshaping their lives with little ones in tow, or the career professional ready to commit further to ambitions in vocation.

Optimal Timing:

Meditate early in the morning to bring about prosperity and health throughout your day. Prosperity spells are best done before the sun rises or while it is still rising. Springtime, dawn, and on Sundays are great times to be inspired for this meditation spell to work best.

Gods/Goddesses:

Isis is the Goddess of abundance. As the Egyptian Goddess of life, Isis is connected to the sun, milk, roses, and bread. We can offer her these things to encourage her help during this meditation. Her influence is associated with fertility and the element of water, thus making her a nurturer and a creator. Her magick can assist in boosting this spell to create healthier and happier results.

Ingredients:

One medium-sized crystal point tower. You can choose which one you like best but here today we start with clear quartz, the Master Initiator stone.

Essential oil of bergamot as its aroma inspires vitality and promotes prosperity and long life.

Almonds

Instructions:

Clear your mind and stand in front of your altar. Place two or three drops of the essential oil onto the crystal and allow it to dry. Let the fragrance infuse the air you breathe.

Sprinkle out the almonds as you ask Isis to join you. *Isis, please accept my wish to prosper and succeed!*

After about a minute of silence, the crystal will be dry, and you can hold it in your hand. Tap the crystal five times with your fingernails to verify its hardness, then recite: *Days to months and months to years. Success we reap without tears. A life content with partnerships, I enjoy success and feel equipped.*

Sit and peacefully envision your life in the next five years earning promotions and significant payments in your favor. Thank Isis for her help. *Isis, thank you for your gracious abundance.* Put away your items and cleanse your space.

Place the crystal somewhere important to you, perhaps on a bookshelf or as a bookend in a display case. If you ever feel yourself declining, meditate again with the stone, tap five times, envisioning the plentiful life you desire.

Tracy Addams

Mental Health Tea Spell

In our modern lives, we are often faced with stresses that tempt us to give up. Our mental health is tested in ways that demand logical recuperative efforts to refrain from trying to be invincible. This simple lemon balm tea spell can calm your adrenals, reducing the release of stressful cortisol hormones. Combined with lavender tea, it will free you of distraction while paving the way for your goals to be achieved.

Optimal Timing:

This spell will have the most benefits when performed during the waxing crescent moon. At this time in the lunar cycle new light is quelling old doubts. This spell is a subtle and relieving one that does not need the power of a full moon to work well. Also, creating this spell at dawn will help to further connect with Brigid, the Celtic Goddess of health that we will invite.

Gods/Goddesses:

The Celtic Goddess Brigid is a patroness of poetry and healing. With her connection to water, Brigid is the perfect Goddess to work with as she powerfully commands the sexual waters within us. She is associated with fire as well and demonstrates her balance of masculine/feminine needs. Brigid is also a fertility Goddess who oversees births and ensures their success. We can offer Brigid her favorites of the season of spring, to which her festival of Imbolc is held.

Ingredients:

Lavender loose leaf tea

Lemon balm loose leaf tea

Tea strainer

Cup and spoon

Boiling water

Yellow candle

Freshly picked shamrocks

Instructions:

In your kitchen, clear your space as you ask Brigid to oversee the making of your healing tea. *Brigid, command these waters to be pure in your name.* Lay out the shamrocks as an offer to Brigid.

Light the yellow candle for a boost in happiness and comfort.

Place the lavender and lemon balm loose tea into the tea strainer and pray: *Leaves and water, warm and serene. Relax my soul and bring sweet dreams.*

Add the water to the leaves and strain the tea after a few minutes. Write these affirmations in a journal in red or blue ink, maybe a mixture of both. *I am mighty, I am bright, I shine gloriously in the afterlife.*

Allow it to steep as you think about a stress-free day. You can also perform this before bed for better sleep. After the tea has cooled a little, sip on it slowly until you smile in serenity. The spell is successful.

Leave the candle to burn as you drink the tea. Once finished, extinguish the candle and pray. *Brigid, I am better having had your help, thank you.*

Chapter 11

Protection and Grounding

One of the original reasons for many people to take up witchcraft is to realize love in phenomenal ways! However, love requires vulnerability and vulnerability puts us at risk of danger. Just as there are physical dangers, we too have spiritual dangers. Black magicians aim to convince us of hurting others and try to sabotage love magick with arrogance, pestilence, and ill will. Protection spells invoke the magnificent power of the Gods and Goddess to remedy and disarm such fools! The initiatic path of witchcraft has protection procedures of seals, banishments, and groundings. These spells release stress and prepare us to defend ourselves with practical measures no different than if we are in the physical house calling 911 to report a complaint.

Protection Jar Spell

A protection jar spell is perfect for keeping in your home to ward off Harpies. Harpies are spiritual messengers of Hades who cast guilt and judgment when carrying ill-fated souls to the confines of hell – they smell of putrid rotting flesh and sound even worse. This protection jar keeps the Harpies at bay when they come to your door, turning them away.

Optimal Timing:

Protection spells are best done during the full moon. This allows your spell to persuade the Harpies to feel dismayed as their justifications are unfounded and illogical. With a spell like this at the full moon you can help defend the home and hearth of other witches too, alleviating the suffering of those you love.

Gods/Goddesses:

The Egyptian Goddess Bastet is the perfect Deity to invite while creating this jar spell. She offers protection and good health to those who welcome her. As a fierce protector of the home, Bastet is depicted as a feline, and as such, she enjoys things related to the number four.

Ingredients:

Four Black candles

Obsidian chips

Tiger's eye chips

Tracy Addams

Dried black pepper

Patchouli essential oil

Small glass jar with a cork

Leather, hemp, or string

Pentagram charm

Fresh catnip sprigs

Instructions:

Warm the obsidian in your right hand, Tiger's Eye in your left. Implore Bastet as you pray: *Bastet, I prepare this jar to protect my house from harm, help me now.*

Begin assembling your jar. Add the warm chips to the jar until it is full as you say, *I forgive you for judging me and I release you.*

Light the four candles and pray: *Only the pure of heart may enter here.*

Drip some melted wax over the cork as you seal the jar, and while it's warm sprinkle the black pepper into the wax. *I am armored to protect myself and those I love.*

Drop at least eight drops of the patchouli essential oil to remedy the foul smell of the Harpies.

Tie your charm around the neck of the jar.

Close your spell by reminding Bastet of your request of her. *Bastet, guard my life with this jar of protection.* Extinguish the candle, then clean up your space.

Keep the jar near the door you most often use to enter your house or home.

Tracy Addams

Protection Blanket Spell

Creating a protection blanket spell is a simple, yet highly beneficial spell to cast. With the element of fire, we manipulate our energies to be untouchable and protect ourselves with the healing power of a blanket. This simple phenomenon of enchantment is useful when we are preyed upon by the evil cerberus with three heads. This blanket of protection surrounds you as you go about your day even when you leave it at home.

Optimal Timing:

This spell doesn't require a specific lunar phase, as it is perfect for quick, on-the-spot protection. It does help, however, to perform this spell in the light of day. Connecting with the sun and its powerful and positive rays will really help to fortify your sensibilities amidst threats.

Gods/Goddesses:

Keep your head held high, because we are asking the help of Apollo, a God of protection, light, music, and knowledge. Because of his strength and order, Apollo is a proud and noble protector of the home. His energies will charge your blanket with the reflective qualities of the sun's solar rays. Apollo enjoys music, laurel wreaths, and golden colored objects, and the bay leaf is sacred to him.

Ingredients:

Gold, silver, glittery, shiny candle

Candle holder

Flat altar dish

Favorite blanket

Bay leaves

Instructions:

Wrap yourself in your blanket, and leave your arms to work in front of you. Invite Apollo to your side as you set out the bay leaves around the dish encircling the candle. *Apollo, protect me and my person, my body and my spirit with all your might.*

Light the candle and say: *Apollo, charge my blanket with the radiant powers of the sun.*

Walk around the candle once and turn your back to it until the blanket has been exposed to the rays of light.

Continue with your intentions and pray: *Protect me and my home from the unwanted. Cerberus, I banish you from this place.*

You can now thank Apollo for watching over you. *Apollo, I thank you for letting me pass.*

To end this protection, fold the blanket and place it at the foot of your bed or in the linen closet. Pickup the bay leaves and recite softly to yourself as you place them outside: *The earth returns to the sky.*

Protective Door Charm Spell

If you're looking to add a lasting spell to your home, especially one that stops evil and negativity in its tracks, this spell is perfect for you. We are working specifically with the rejection of the Celtic Leprechaun, a treacherous evil spirit. Don't be fooled by his employment in public spaces, Leprechauns are minor spirits who need to emerge from poor behavior. By enchanting your item, then hanging it on or around your front door, you will be preventing such thieving, cheating, and lying spirits from entering your home. Best yet, this spell can be cast on something you already use on your door, so that it never draws attention or clashes with your décor.

Optimal Timing:

This protection spell is best done when energies are strong and high. During the full moon, during midday when the sun is most bright, or in the middle of the week are all perfect times. We should understand that the Leprechaun aims to deceive and trick you into manipulating your emotions which makes you drop your guard.

Gods/Goddesses:

To protect your home from unwanted energies, there really is no better Goddess than Hestia. As the Greek Goddess of the hearth and home, Hestia's focus is on the family and their growth, and because of this, she is a very practical protector and watcher for those in the home. Hestia is associated with the harvest as well as family gatherings, and she enjoys offerings of the harvest such as fruits, nuts, bread, milk, and honey.

Ingredients:

Favorite door décor item (wreaths, doorknock or chime, sigils, etc)

Seven short candles (assortment of green and red)

Coarse salt

Sage smudge bundle

Heat-resistant plate

Cow or goat milk to drink

Instructions:

Begin by finding a large enough place to cast a sacred circle. Lay out your items in the middle of the circle before you cast it.

Set out the milk and invite Hestia to join you. *Hestia, protect me from trickery and guide me ahead in life.*

Set your décor item in the center of your circle, then place the candles around the item in the shape of a seven pointed star, and light them.

Light the sage bundle from the candles and wave the smoke over the décor item to cleanse it and give it purpose. Ash out the sage in the dish and add the salt to the ashes, making a pinch of black salt.

Speak your intentions like this: *Remove and banish the wicked and rude. Protect this home with love and virtue.*

Take the black salt between your hand and sprinkle it over the décor item, sealing it with this rune Sig. Hiss like a snake three times, ssssss, sssss, sssss, and pray: *Hestia hear me, please. You now protect this home and your wisdom is venerated.*

The wisdom of the serpent is to rise and drink the elixir of long life, so now drink the milk, a symbol of virtue. Thank Hestia for her participation. *Hestia, thank you for teaching me this virtue of wisdom.*

Extinguish the candles and close your circle. Hang your décor item on your front door. You are now enlightened to the true wisdom of spiritual fulfillment, and will no longer be fascinated by the unlikely charms of the Leprechaun.

Meditative Banishing Spell

When negative feelings overwhelm us and we start to lose pace of ourselves, there very well could be unwanted energies haunting us. We must understand this sentiment may be caused by the ravenous Fenrir, a giant Norse wolf who brought much havoc to the Gods by bullying and inducing fear over his size and howls to the moon. A meditative banishing spell is just the cure. The easiest way to make this happen is by using incantations with a powerful cubic crystal under moonlight.

Optimal Timing:

Banishing spells are best done during the waning phases of the moon. As the moon is coming down from its superior glow, we can use its releasing energy to remove things that we no longer want. A waning moon allows us to forgive and forget, treat illnesses, and starve old habits that are not helping us anymore.

Gods/Goddesses:

The Hindu Goddess Kali is perfect for this banishing spell. She is known to hold the power of transformation, reaching beyond the normal constructs of life itself. She is the illustrious invigorator who invokes true change, helping us to see in the darkness, with a twilight of hope. In addition, Kali is known to destroy the demons of our minds who trouble us. Kali is often given red hibiscus flowers, which are her favorite, as well as rice and lentils.

Ingredients:

Small cauldron

Hematite cube(s)

Tracy Addams

Water and drinking cup

A handful of rice

Instructions:

Find a quiet place to sit with a table or altar in front of you. Summon the Goddess Kali by putting rice in the cauldron. *Kali, help me to destroy and eliminate my fears of the unknown.*

Relax for ten minutes or more, as you see the almighty Kali with her ten heads, ten arms, and ten legs, swinging her swords and other implements defeating the angry Fenrir, piercing him in the heart.

Holding the cubic hematite in your left hand, get up and prepare some moon water with your right by pouring the water into the drinking cup and setting it under moonlight overnight.

The hematite has helped you set your intentions, now set it on the little bed of rice under the cauldron lid and pray: *I use this hematite to feel protected from all sides by the Gods above.*

You are feeling recharged and confident, just remember to drink the moonwater in the morning.

Thank Kali for helping: *Goddess Kali, my messenger of destruction, I thank you.*

Grounding Roller Ball Medley

Protection helps us to safeguard ourselves from trauma, grief, and worry. Sometimes, however, we might already be carrying those negative emotions with us as a result of the hardship we feel in weighing severity from mercy. Such is the work of Ra, the Sun God, who every night has to find victory by decapitating the evil serpent Apep, who was born from Ra's own shadow. Our own shadow, the part of us we are learning to transform into an intuitive source of inspiration, needs to be cared for. If not, the burdens of life - trauma, grief and worry - won't allow us to absorb the beautiful rays of sunshine we expect to find everyday. Being able to quickly ground ourselves will help to remedy those undigested energies to keep focus and stand tall.

Optimal Timing:

Casting this spell does not require a specific timing. But because the medley will help to keep you grounded, you may choose to perform this spell during the waning moon phase to capture its releasing energy. Likewise, you may want to use the heightened energy of the full moon to increase the power of the medley. This is up to you as the timing is not as important as the recipe itself.

Gods/Goddesses:

As an Earth Goddess, Gaia is ideal to help ground us and relieve unnatural stresses from our lives. She is the Greek Goddess known as Mother Earth and embodies fertility and life in all its forms. Gaia is a beloved Goddess who guides us in the way a mother would as a nurturer. She enlightens and protects, and she keeps us firm in who we are. Gaia is connected to all things of the forest, especially deeply scented wood like cedar, hickory, and sandalwood.

Tracy Addams

Ingredients:

Sandalwood essential oil

Bergamot essential oil

Juniper essential oil

Wild orange essential oil

Carrier oil (such as olive oil, almond oil, jojoba oil or avocado oil)

10 ml roller ball bottle

Daisy flowers to offer Gaia

Instructions:

Clean a flat surface and lay out all your ingredients. Offer Gaia the daisies and ask her to cast the spell together. *Gaia, please join your words with mine–let me succeed and my worries fade.*

Begin by adding nine drops of each essential oil to the bottle. As you do this, speak the following words. *Sandalwood connects me to the tides–Ocean's heavy, hold me tight. Bergamot drifting on the breeze–Winds light, truly free. Juniper firm with roots below–Keep me grounded as my spirit grows. Orange so bright and oh so sweet–Like the fire under Heaven's feet.*

Now add enough carrier oil to finish off the bottle. Place the roller ball on top to seal in the recipe..

Finish by thanking Gaia for her help. *Gaia, thank you for keeping my hand steady, head high, and heart calm.*

Now you can clean your items and begin rolling the medley on your head, arms, and legs as you see fit.

Tracy Addams

Witchcraft Magick Spells

Chapter 12

Success and Leadership

Becoming successful is a result of exerting significant practical efforts in our lives. Success to you might involve your career, your relationship with your spouse, or the relationship with your family. Success to each of us is becoming an independent individual, but we can manifest success in any area of our lives beyond this so that we can rise above defeatism to become the leaders we know we can be. Witches are natural leaders, often taking their own path in life and rejecting intellectualism as blind faith by seeking intuitive pathways. We are seekers of knowledge, experiential knowledge, questioning everything as we try to find a deeper understanding of life itself. The success that you seek in any area of your life is obtainable thanks to the wonders of our inner nature.

Success Jar Spell

Finding success might seem like a difficult task, but with some good magick, we can take advantage of circumstances and use persuasion to achieve positive outcomes! This jar spell is perfect for helping you find new business opportunities, and it may also lead to sales or leadership opportunities. Success can also come in many forms. If you're wanting to reach an achievement in your personal life, this jar spell can work wonders to discover new passions or find innovative ideas.

Optimal Timing:

With success spells, we are looking to get more of what we know we want, consistently. This means it is best to perform this spell during the waxing phase of the moon's cycle. In addition, we may also want to create this spell in the morning to amplify it along with the growing light of the sun. Finally, springtime is great for creating success jars as it is a time when the world is flourishing with energy under Mother Nature's abundant fertility.

Gods/Goddesses:

As the Greek Goddess of intelligence and war, Athena knows how to succeed. Athena's support in this jar spell will help to infuse majestic magick with your innate power. She is a well-balanced Goddess whose loyalty and craftiness can help guide anyone in reaching their achievements. Athena is connected to the dark moon, and thus giving her offerings at this time can help gain her trust. She enjoys roses, olives, wheat grains, and blue or sea-themed trinkets.

Ingredients:

Pink candle

Small jade stone

Citrine crystal chips

Dried cinnamon

Frankincense essential oil

Small glass jar with a cork

Leather, hemp, or string

Pentagram charm

Rose petals

Instructions:

Pull off a few rose petals from a fresh rose and taste their bitter flavor in your mouth with a few chews. Place the soggy petals into the jar and remember, Athena loves to be worshiped. *Athena, oh heralded warrior so mighty, guide me through your successful ways.*

Remember Athena fights for the virgin, so light your candle and recite like this: *To honor the innocent words spoken from the mouth of the virgin, I offer bright new opportunities to be a magnet for success.*

Begin assembling your jar spell. Add the small jade to the jar as you say: *I am full of charisma.*

Sprinkle the cinnamon into the jar and over the malachite. *I am ready for success.*

Add the citrine chips. *I am in command of myself.*

Drop in ten drops of the frankincense essential oil. *My spirit is bound to success.*

Close the jar with a cork and pray: *I command you, Athena, to seal this jar.*

Tie your pentacle around the neck of the jar. Melt your pink candle wax over the cork to create a permanent seal. Continue with your intentions and pray: *I rise to succeed, I rise to success, I feel harmony, I feel my best.*

Let Athena know she is divine in every way. *Athena, I am a part of your work, my success is your success, thank you.*

Extinguish the candle and then cleanse your space.

Tracy Addams

Keep the jar on your altar to improve your spells, at work to realize your career potential, in your purse to find your rebellious nature, or buried in the earth in your backyard to increase your property value.

Success and Power (S&P) Fan Spell

Making affirmations that increase our confidence and boost our abilities to achieve our goals is exactly what it means to become successful. This simple fan spell is a perfect way to enhance your success and power in any aspect of your life. When reversed, this is a binding spell which should be performed if the witch encounters troubles.

Optimal Timing:

This fan spell can be done at any moment before you are about to take a test. It also works well before going out to attend a gathering where you know you will need confidence and charisma to fully enjoy the moment. I recommend you pull a Tarot card, or three, read them, and leave them fanned out on your altar to weigh your options. Your understanding of the reading should be considered with the lightheartedness of a feather and the humor of the funny bone.

Gods/Goddesses:

The Aztec God Quetzelcoatl is the amazing feathered serpent who brings together wind and rain to help create humanity as we know it. He invented the calendar and works with the morning star Venus, and he loves education and learning, especially with children. Quetzelcoatl waited 600 years to learn his lessons to help humanity. He enjoys black and yellow feathers and the smell of coffee.

Ingredients:

Feathered fan

Open air bag full of coffee beans

Tracy Addams

78-card Tarot deck

Instructions:

Before getting out of bed, pull your fan from its drawer or safe place on the wall and observe the breeze on your cheeks. Smell the coffee beans as you ask Quetzalcoatl to dress you in the Solar Robes of the soul. *Quetzalcoatl, adorn me brightly and do so rightly.*

Now, ever-so-sweetly, meditate on the sound of the word *ohm* as you chant it.

Speak this mantra three times and return the fan to its original place at your bedside. *Success is mine, from this day onward. Wind and rain, wind and rain, I let my sorrows go down the drain.*

Tie a white ribbon around the bag of beans if you are struggling emotionally to pass this test of confidence. This binding will fully dispel any attack that Quetzalcoatl is teaching you to overcome.

Tyr of Victory Enchantment Spell

This spell is the perfect way to enchant any item you use in your profession. The item will become imbued with the power of success and future achievements, possibly landing you that promotion or new pay raise you're after.

Optimal Timing:

This enchantment spell will have the most power if it is performed during the waxing or full moon. It will gather the growing energy of the moon and enable you to find victory over any feelings of self-doubt, especially in the affairs of the heart.

Gods/Goddesses:

While the Norse God Tyr sacrificed his arm to help defeat the wolf Fenrir, he taught us his humble rune which holds his name, the Rune Tyr. Before going to bed, we will invoke Tyr and ask him to guide our Astral body through the night to teach us the ways of the Gods and Goddesses. Having him help in this enchantment can open new doors to you and allow you to find the victory you so desire. Tyr is a God of War, so we fast in his honor, and feast after Victory.

Ingredients:

An important item–favorite pen, handbag, or love jar spell.

A chair to sit in

Instructions:

Tyr is a warrior so he respects simplicity. Sit in your chair and relax your mind until it is understood you can begin. Stand up on your feet and cup your hands at your side with straight arms. Lift your arms above your head and recite this mantra: *Tyyyyyyyyrrrrrrrrr* as you slowly bring your arms to your thighs, seeing the object infused with the vibrations of your tongue channeled by the air you cup in your hands. Remember to roll the rrrrr as your tongue vibrates in your mouth.

You have brought your body through the shape of the Rune, Tyr, or letter T, significantly represented by the arrows that pierce the backside of future lovers sent from cupid's bow.

Rest easy overnight, and pray softly as you drift to sleep: *Power, vigor, life, and light. Raise success and lift my might.*

Meditative Leadership Tea Spell

Even when opportunity seems to be at our doorstep, we might find ourselves requiring more patience to see how to advance successfully. Confidence can be found with practice, but as a booster, a spot of clove tea with the right affirmations can convince any narrow-mindedness we have just how capable we truly are to step through the door.

Optimal Timing:

Meditation is great any time of the day, and it eventually becomes a walking lifestyle. Engaging in challenging affairs requires careful focus and determination, qualities we develop in meditation. But we should take charge of our life –we should spring into action. This spell should be done every Ostara, especially by the Cosmic witch, under the light of the full moon.

Gods/Goddesses:

The Hindu Lord Ganesha is the perfect Deity to help us mark the occasion. He is known to remove obstacles and make it easier for a prosperous life to take hold. His big belly enjoys being tickled and his elephant head full of memory waits for children to come of age, adults to become parents, and elders to become grandparents. Those opportunities that are hiding just out of sight will become clear with his helpful wisdom and foresight.

Ingredients:

Purple fluorite crystal

Washbasin

Two cloves in moon water

Tracy Addams

Instructions:

Cloves are a pungent spice that dries the mouth and heats up anyone's metabolism. We should place the cup of hot moon water on the table with both cloves inside it on the altar to infuse.

Then pray like this: *Lord Ganesha, with my two eyes and my two ears. My two hands and my two feet. My two legs and my two arms. I surrender them all to my spirit. With this one cup, I ask you to give me strength in leadership.*

Hold the purple fluorite in your hands and wash it in the basin underwater. This stone represents your spiritual path and should take prominence on your altar for its ability to open the pineal gland. Your pineal gland is the lotus of one-thousand petals that illuminates the mind with the creative potency of the sexual organs.

Continue praying until the purple fluorite is washed clean: *Stone so bright, bring my wishes to light. Successes I seek, so mote it be.*

Seriously thank Ganesha for his presence. *Ganesha, you are my crown of wisdom.* Drink the moon water leaving the two cloves at the bottom of the cup and dispense them as you wish.

Charismatic Energizing Tonic/Tincture/Tea

This soothing tonic is the perfect confidence booster for any morning or nighttime routine. You can use it to add some charismatic vibes to your day as you head out toward success. Bonus, it improves oral health, helps with menstrual cramps, and assists in milk production for breastfeeding.

Optimal Timing:

The witch who understands alchemy will brew vervain in her kitchen as a tonic, tincture, or tea, or all three. Vervain should be taken in addition to regular food and drink, either as an additive tonic to a full glass of water, a few drops under the tongue as a tincture or simply infused as a ready-made tea. We will also add hibiscus to sweeten it up, and passionflower to balance it out. This combination of herbs helps to promote deep sleep, reduces anxiety, and relieves pains and spasms.

Gods/Goddesses:

The Greek God Dionysus is known for being confident and charismatic. With his knowledge of vegetation and wine and his boastful desires for ecstasy and orgies, Dionysus reminds us to be chaste in respecting our emotional health. His sacred offerings include pine cones, ivy, and grapes.

Ingredients for the Tincture:

Blue vervain dried flowers (3 tablespoons)

Hibiscus dried flowers (3 tablespoons)

Passionflowers, dried (3 tablespoons)

Mason jar(s)

Tracy Addams

Glycerin (1 cup, food-grade)

Boiling water (1 cup)

Instructions (just multiply the measurement for multiple jars):

Lay out the grapes as you invite Dionysus to join you in the kitchen. *Dionysus, help me measure and mix.*

As you add the nine tablespoons of flowers, perform this mantra four times over: *From the Earth to my soul, lively spirit, brave and bold.*

Fill the jar(s) ⅓ full with boiling water, and tamp down the flowers with the spoon. Add in the glycerin until the jar(s) is near full and cover with a lid. Place the jar(s) into a cooktop ⅓ the way full of water and cover with another lid. Ensure there is some fabric at the bottom to avoid damaging the jars with too much heat. Monitor the water level as it simmers for a day. Feel free to shake the jars to extract the healing juices from the flowers. Strain the flowers from the jars using a cheesecloth and find the beautiful red hued liquid tincture. Place it in amber bottles with appropriate labels and keep it in the fridge for anytime for family use.

Thank Dionysus for his involvement. *Dionysus, this tincture is perfect, thank you.*

Chapter 13

Wealth and Abundance

Becoming financially secure is a great goal of many witches. We all want to know that our money troubles will go away and that we will be able to live a comfortable life taking care of all the witches we love most. Finding wealth and abundance is possible through spell casting as a practical means. Take advantage of new fortunes and increased riches with the abundance and overflow of the potential we are about to unveil.

Wealth Smudge and Smoke

The era of poverty of the spirit is gone—wealth should find its abundance in our lives. This combination of resins I am about to offer reduces to ashes any mystery about acquiring wealth in every corner of a witch's life. Fundamental to every witch's practice is the alchemy behind the mystery of the philosophical stone of sex, for which we need to be hermetic. The steams of passion need to boil and rise from the foundation to the crown to illuminate the witch for a complete awakening of her spirit. It is love that guides the smudge and smoke to let the miracles of every day reach the corners of every room of our house, cleansing and welcoming wealth in abundance.

Optimal Timing:

Perform this wealth smudge and smoke as often as you wish, especially to christen a new home or after a long journey. Every sabbat should include a wealth smudge and smoke so a family or coven doesn't forget their financial responsibilities to each other.

Gods/Goddesses:

The Hindu Goddess Lakshmi is the Goddess of wealth and good fortune. As a Goddess, Lakshmi is also bestowed with grace and charm, helping her husband Vishnu raise the five serpents to commune together with Brahma. She helps him dominate his desires as a Mistress of the magickal waters. Lakshmi is a graceful and lovely Deity who shares her splendor when she is revered properly.

Ingredients:

Blue or white candle

Tracy Addams

Incense carrier big enough for a charcoal puck

Guggul resin (India type)

Copal resin (golden quality)

Instructions:

Clean the cup and place the puck inside, lips face up. Address Lakshmi like this: *Lakshmi, endow me with immaculate wealth and abundance.*

Light the candle and speak your intentions. *With this candle, I welcome the riches of my sacred fires.*

Tip the candle in to light the puck, careful not to spill any wax – it's ok if you do a little bit. Let the puck pass five minutes of burning, and place a few bits of resin on top of it.

Walk in a clockwise direction within your home, being careful to spread the smoke into every room, closet, and corner. Once the space is completely cleansed, leave the container to burn out on a table or deck. Do not add water until it cools.

Finish your invocation to Lakshmi with a goodbye. *Lakshmi, pure heart, pure mind, with love so kind, I reap the wealth of what is mine.*

Abundance Candle Spell

This spell works quickly to draw money and good fortune into your life. We combine this candle spell with five cards of Tarot, three-high, two-low. High: past, present, future. Low: reason, potential.

Optimal Timing:

This spell is best done when the moon is full and high. Abundance spells are intended to be a time to manifest and set your goals to let them grow and flourish with amazing results. Anytime you face heightened energy, hype, or pressure to deliver ideas, cast this spell to enter into creative harmony, and watch as frustrations wash away.

Gods/Goddesses:

The Celtic God Cernunnos is revered as the God of wealth, but he not only represents it, he is known for spreading it. Cernunnos is connected to the wild natural forests of northern Europe, as his horns depict. This God is also believed to be the God of the underworld, from where the ancients believed riches came from. This is actually very true since both gold and other priceless materials do come from deep in the earth's crust. Cernunnos can be offered things associated with the material bounties of the earth to show respect.

Ingredients:

Green candle

Coconut oil

Cinnamon

Carving tool (toothpicks, pencils, clay tools, or athame)

Tracy Addams

Salty seeds like dill, parsley & basil

78-card Tarot deck

Instructions:

Find a quiet place where you can focus and be left alone.

Pull five cards and place them on a table to read. Intuit your relationship with the past, set goals for the future, and understand your present intentions, with reason for potential wealth. *Cernunnos, fill my spirit with the wealth I so abundantly visualize.*

Holding your candle, carve your name into the wax.

Apply coconut oil to the carving, then sprinkle cinnamon over the oil so that it sticks and brings your name to life. Cinnamon is perfect at aiding in money and wealth, while coconut oil revitalizes with its yummy aroma.

Light the candle as you repeat this enchantment three times: *Money, money, steady, strong. Plentiful money come along.*

Finish by spilling the seeds into the air out a window, or planting them in your garden to grow for your kitchen. *Cernunnos, as these seeds die and are born into plants, so am I born with them.*

Extinguish the candle for later or let it burn to its base.

Wealth Sigil Spell

Carrying your wealth with you will allow you to be open to new opportunities for financial growth. This could mean new job openings, coming across a fantastic investment, or inventing something new and innovative, something you regard as a treasure.

Optimal Timing:

You can perform this sigil spell once a month, and I wouldn't recommend any more than that. Of course, as with other money spells, doing this during the waxing moon will increase your chances of abundance and plentiful results.

Gods/Goddesses:

Ploutos is the Greek God of wealth and harvest. He is depicted as a young boy with a cornucopia in his hands. His overflowing wealth can aid in this spell as you put your energy into the sigil. As a boy, he hasn't entered into the realm of water magick, also known as sexual magick. Being a harvest Deity, he relies on irrigation, so Ploutos receives offerings associated with rivers, lake,s and rains.

Ingredients:

Material to draw on, paper

Pen

Ten candles, any mixture of colors

River, lake, or rain water

Tracy Addams

Instructions:

Find yourself decided and prepared to enter a wealthy lifestyle, resplendent in abundance. Ploutos will come when you inspire him to, but you can pray anyways. *Ploutos, I invite you into my life.*

Light all ten candles. Relax as you sketch out your sigil for wealth. Your sigil is a map for your intuition to follow with Ploutos awarding you the immersion into wealth beyond measure. It is perfect exactly as you draw it.

Combine this sigil with anything you want to bring you closer to wealth and financial stability. It can be sewn onto a handbag, painted onto a keepsake for a desk, or etched into a candle for you to burn. There are many ways to include the sigil in your career and personal life.

Conclude the spell by extinguishing the candles and thanking the boy God or his help. *Plutous, protect my wealth on this day and forever.*

Meditative Good Fortune Spell

Witches study the vibrations of certain gemstones which manifest wealth in order to reframe our mindset about money. The reason we do this is because money flows like a river, ebbing with the tides, and flooding with the rains. Water tumbled stones offer us so much wisdom, reshaping themselves to abide comfortably, immersed in an abundance of water. Good fortune in the world of wealth doesn't come to those who merely pray–we are divining our spirit for action!

Optimal Timing:

This meditative spell can be performed anytime as it is meant to constantly increase the value of our possessions. Confidence in making grand decisions requires us to value the possessions we already have. The use of a tumbled stone, either natural or machine tumbled, is a great way to start. Take your tumbled stone with you, or wear it as jewelry to stay in touch with your intentions. The infusion we take to manage the changes in or gut chemistry is marjoram.

Gods/Goddesses:

The Goddess Fortuna from the Roman pantheon is associated with fortune, chance, and fate. She is linked to the season of summer, bringing bounties of early harvests of wildberries and rosemary. Fortuna has many depictions, many wearing a blindfold. To win her favor, it's best to feed her with song and merriment.

Ingredients:

Tumbled peridot or carnelian

Wind chime or bell

Tracy Addams

Marjoram tea

Pentacle

Instructions:

Infuse some Marjoram tea to smell as you prepare the spell, and drink when you are done. *Fortuna, I possess this gemstone, washed pure, as my own.*

Ring the bell or rattle the chimes as you say: *Abundant riches come to me, with this sound, I summon thee.*

Hold the gemstone closer to your heart, and pray like this: *Money and wealth protect me, this I cast, so mote it be.*

After you are filled with visions of all the wealth you desire, and are happy about your intentions, drink your tea and remark how grateful you are for all of your possessions. *Thank you, Fortuna, for enlightening me to what I am capable of.*

Keep the stone in the northern part of your home on a pentagram to seal the magick. Gnomes of the Earth respond to northern orientations and will work to your benefit.

Treasure Finder Balm

Balms are great for many reasons. Not only do they naturally sooth your chapped or dry skin, but you can also infuse them with essential oils endowed by the sacred elementals living within the flowers. This balm recipe is great for any day, but it's truly perfect for interviews and business meetings. It permits the skin of your spirit, your personality, to glow under the resplendency of your intuition. Green witches might want to use fresh herbs from their own garden after butterflies have visited.

Optimal Timing:

This balm can be applied at any time you need, but under the darkness of a new moon when the stars are brightest, you will be most inspired.

Gods/Goddesses:

Tracy Addams

Asking Njord (pronounced Ni-your-rrrd, with a rolled R), the Norse God of the wind, sea, and riches, to help in this spell is the perfect fit. Njord is known to bestow wealth upon his followers through the wisdom of the sea.

Ingredients:

Mason jar with a lid

Shea butter

Beeswax

Coconut oil

Jojoba oil

Vitamin E oil

Lily essential oil

Calendula essential oil

Popsicle stir stick

Sea salt

Instructions:

Set out all of your items on a clean surface and sprinkle some salt inside the mason jar. Rinse it with water. *Njord, see my love of wealth and help me to foster it in abundance.*

Recite these words: *Treasures appear before my eyes, that I may have a plentiful life. No harm shall come to anyone, this is my will, and now it is done.*

Add three tablespoons of shea butter, one tablespoon of beeswax, and one tablespoon of coconut oil to the microwavable mason jar. Microwave on low heat for fifteen seconds at a time, until the mixture is melted. Use the stir stick in between intervals.

Immediately after, because the mixture will be thick and hard as it cools, add in three tablespoons of jojoba oil and one teaspoon of vitamin E oil.

Pour the mixture into a tiny container if you have one or keep it in the mason jar. This recipe makes about two ounces.

Add ten drops of Lily essential oil and ten drops of Calendula essential oil for a total of 20 drops. Stir the balm in the jar with the popsicle stick while it's still soft.

Once it cools, which takes about two hours, you can use the balm in your daily routine to set your skin aglow to attract wealth. Continue to use it daily until it is completely used up–this should be at least three months' worth for the spell to take full effect.

Thank Njord for supporting you at this time. *Njord, see my skin as a treasure of the spirit.*

Tracy Addams

Witchcraft Magick Spells

Conclusion

Practice Makes Perfect

We all have the ability to become magickal and live incredible lives. We can build a strong connection to the occult faculties within us and use those energies to help us invoke positive change. As witches, we succeed in protecting, loving, healing, and teaching others the way of our ancestors. As we do it wholeheartedly, with the responsibility of leading the next generation, we hand down these sacred traditions through intuitive means.

The beauty of finding your spiritual place in this life is that you can begin to work on the real you. You'll accept yourself with all your soul, allowing old wounds to heal and new connections to form. Magick is a practice. We learn and grow as we travel through our lives, picking up new information as we meet others and learn their ways. Humanity can only become stronger as we work together to reach our potential and unite with our cosmic nature.

We practice magick because the mystery of life and death inspires us to. There is so much to learn about the natural world, as our physical eyes obey the laws of the physical world, we have learned how our spiritual eyes obey the laws of the spiritual world. These spells we perform are done using the language of the heart, with symbols, numbers, and images, we have awakened the consciousness inside us. Witches bring purpose to their everyday lives, intuitively gathering and manipulating energies to enlighten and enrich humanity. In witchcraft, we learn that we are capable of great things and that we have the power to follow the path of initiation.

To all the witches who have discovered this book, I am glad to have helped you to learn more about witchcraft and the wonders of magick. I hope that you revel in your practice and that you find many amazing and enlightening experiences throughout your life. I thank you for allowing me to connect with you through our shared passions and beliefs. Feel free to contact

Tracy Addams

me at <u>tracy.addams@intuitive-way.com</u> or through our website and private Facebook group Intuitive Way Publishing.

All witches everywhere are unique and beautiful–we are powerful beyond measure. Blessed be.

Glossary of Terms

Altar: The place where a witch keeps her most important items for ritual worship and spell casting. She may light candles and pray to this altar and the Gods or Goddesses she reveres every day.

Athame: A symbolic and ceremonial blade that witches use during spell casting or rituals.

Banish: The removal of negative or unwelcomed energies, including spirits, hexes, trauma, and guilt.

Bind: The act of connecting two or more things together with magickal influence. One witch can bind another in order to prevent her from doing bad magick. Binding can also bring two people closer. This can be positive or negative.

Cauldron: A symbolic cup, pot, or container that represents the Goddess and her connection to the Earth. The cauldron is often part of an altar, and it symbolizes a womb of growth and fertility. They are often inscribed with personal, powerful sigils.

Coven: A gathering of witches who meet regularly to practice their shared beliefs in witchcraft.

Elemental Signs: The four classic elements, Earth, air, fire, and water. Sometimes a fifth element, the one of spirit, is included.

Equinox: Two specific days in the wheel of the year when the earth receives an equal amount of light and dark. The spring equinox and autumn equinox are the sabbats of Ostara and Mabon, respectively.

Esbats: The lesser holy days of the witch's calendar, comprising principally each full moon, though a new moon may be celebrated as an esbat, as well. In some covens, the word esbat is used to refer to any ritual meeting of witches outside of a sabat, regardless of lunar phase.

Hex: A magickal charm or spell that is intended to cause harm.

Incense: A stick or cone of herbs that is meant to be burned. It releases a favorable scent and often adds to the power of the magick.

Magick: The magick that a witch, particularly one who practices Wicca, uses to craft and cast spells. The added *K* is meant to distinguish the word from theater magic.

Mortar and Pestle: A small bowl and grinding tool used to crush things for spell preparations and medicinal remedies.

Numerology: The study and belief behind numbers having importance, and that each number means something specific to our actions and thoughts.

Pantheon: The respected and revered Gods and Goddesses within a specific religion or spirituality practice.

Potions: A liquid mixture that has magickal powers.

Ritual: A sacred or religious ceremony that is made up of specific actions. Rituals are meant for worship or to bless, and are connected to important events such as Sabbats.

Runes: Oftly misinterpreted as inscribed alphabetic stones. Actually, runes are cosmic mathematical poses that when performed offer a means for divination.

Sabbats: The eight holy days of the witch's wheel of the year, based on the solar calendar and pre-Christian European fire festivals. The sabbats are, in order from the witch's near year, Samhain, Yule, Imbolg, Ostara, Beltane, Litha, Lughnasadh, and Mabon.

Scrying: Using items such as glass and mirrors to see visions from the spirit world.

Sigils: A symbol that is thought to hold magickal power.

Solstice: Two specific days in the wheel of the year when the earth receives a majority of either light or dark. At the summer solstice, also called Litha, the earth receives more light than darkness. During the winter solstice, called Yule, the earth receives more darkness.

Spells: Also called an enchantment or incantation, a spell is a set of words meant to invoke change with the use of magickal power and energy.

Tarot: A deck consisting of 78 cards. The cards are used in divination and are read by a witch or psychic.

Tincture: A highly concentrated form of herbal oil made by soaking plant parts in oils or grain alcohol. They can be added to balms or tonics to increase their efficacy.

Tonic: A drink mixture that is believed to hold healing powers. Tonics are made with herbs and other natural remedies.

Tree of Life: A universal symbol common among many religions both monotheistic and pagan or neopagan. Also known as sephiroth, or churches, the spheres represent advancement in spiritual disciplines in higher dimensions of nature, but also infra dimensions exist.

Wands: A handheld item that a witch will use to cast her spells. It can be bought or made and is often highly personal and reflective of the witch's personality.

Wiccan Rede: The Wiccan code of morals. It provides witches with a basic guide on how magick should be handled.

Warlock: A male practitioner of magick.

Witch: A female practitioner of magick.

#WitchTok: A popular hashtag that witches use to promote their content on #TikTok and other social media. Tied to this is #BookTok, which promotes books in general.

Wheel of the Year: The pagan calendar based on European pre-Christian fire festivals, the solar solstices, and the equinoxes. The wheel of the year begins on Samhain, the witch's new year, and includes seven additional sabbats or major pagan festivals.

Reference

Collections, DMA, *Cultures & Traditions, Ancient Egyptian Beliefs*, Dallas Museum of Art, 2017, https://collections.dma.org/essay/makAzZyl

National Geographic, *Religion According to the Ancient Greeks*, https://www.nationalgeographic.org/media/religion-according-ancient-greeks/#:~:text=The%20ancient%20Greeks%20believed%20that,made%20you%20worthy%20of%20immortality.

Mark, Joshua J., *Ten Norse Mythology Facts You Need to Know*, World History Encyclopedia, September 21, 2021, https://www.worldhistory.org/article/1836/ten-norse-mythology-facts-you-need-to-know/

History.Com Editors, *Who Were Celts*, History.Com, October 24, 2019, https://www.history.com/topics/ancient-history/celts#:~:text=It's%20believed%20that%20the%20Celtic,culture%20are%20still%20prominent%20today.

Lewis, Ioan M., *The Witch Hunts*, Brittanica.Com, https://www.britannica.com/topic/witchcraft/The-witch-hunts

Wigington, Patti, *Biography of Gerald Gardner and the Gardnerian Wiccan Tradition*, Learn Religions, May 13, 2019, https://www.learnreligions.com/what-is-gardnerian-wicca-2562910

Wigington, Patti, *The Triple Goddess: Maiden, Mother and Crone*, January 28, 2019, Learn Religions, https://www.learnreligions.com/maiden-mother-and-crone-2562881

Celtic Gods and Goddesses, Grove of Nova Scotia Druids, https://www.druidry.ca/gods-and-goddesses

Mark, Joshua J., *Egyptian Gods: The Complete List*, April 14, 2016, World History Encyclopedia, https://www.worldhistory.org/article/885/egyptian-gods---the-complete-list/

Greek Gods and Goddesses, Theoi Greek Mythology, https://www.theoi.com/greek-mythology/greek-gods.html

Gods and Creatures, Norse Mythology for Smart People, https://norse-mythology.org/gods-and-creatures/

Irish Central, *Celtic Mythology*, December 30, 2021, https://www.irishcentral.com/roots/history/celtic-mythology-gods-goddesses

Rosson, Kat, *The Kabbalah Tree of Life,* May 3, 2018, Haari Kabbalah Jewelry, https://kabbalah72.net/blogs/kabbalah-news/the-kabbalah-tree-of-life

Wigington, Patti, *Types of Witches,* Learn Religions, October 28, 2019, https://www.learnreligions.com/types-of-witches-4774438

Tarot Meaning Cheat Sheets: Infographics Plus Free Printable Resource, Labyrinthos, December 10, 2018 https://labyrinthos.co/blogs/learn-tarot-with-labyrinthos-academy/tarot-meaning-cheat-sheets-infographics-plus-free-printable-resource

Gemstone Meanings & Crystal Properties, Beadage, https://beadage.net/gemstones/

Fountaine, Sylvia, *Wonder Balm*, December 17, 2020, Feasting at Home, https://www.feastingathome.com/shea-butter-body-balm/#tasty-recipes-41014-jump-target

Aun Weor, Samael, *Curso Zodiacal,* Spanish Version, June 24, 2011, ASIN: B00580JHJW

The Magic of the Runes, July 15, 2018, Gnostic Muse, https://www.gnosticmuse.com/the-magic-of-the-runes/

Tinctures, Tonics, and Teas, July, 7, 2019, The Windesphere Witch

https://stirringthesenses.typepad.com/the_windesphere_witch/tinctures-tonics-teas/

Taste and Action on Chinese Herbs, Traditional and Modern Views, Subhuti Dharmananda, Ph. D.,

http://www.itmonline.org/articles/taste_action/taste_action_herbs.htm

www.ingramcontent.com/pod-product-compliance
Lightning Source LLC
Chambersburg PA
CBHW072049110526
44590CB00018B/3103